"This book has moved me more than almost any other. Alan's childhood daydreaming of influencing thousands has truly come to fruition. This is a compellingly life story written with transparent honesty. It's about a truly authentic man of God. His deep love for the former Soviet Union countries shines emotively through the pages. He comments on the possible futures of these nations' believers and sounds a warning note. Those with a heart for this region should read it."

Derek Copley BSc (Hons) PhD; *Global Connections Council Member and chair of the UK Central Asia Forum, Former Chair of EAUK, the European Evangelical Alliance (EEA), and Principal of Moorlands College*

"My friendship with Alan grew when we were both church leaders. In him I saw glimpses of the manner and character of Jesus, the One he had believed in and followed as a disciple since his childhood. He who God calls, He equips. With a heart filled with compassion and care to serve suffering people throughout the world, it was no surprise to me that the Holy Spirit led Alan to serve the ministry of Samaritan's Purse around the world."

Rev Mike Pusey; *former Pastor, Millmead Baptist Church, Guildford. Speaker and early influencer in the UK Charismatic Church Movement. Pioneer of Professional Football Club chaplaincies, and Aldershot Town FC chaplain.*

"Many themes run through this story. One is the outworking of the love of the Father, the hope which is Jesus our Lord and the power of the Holy Spirit. It has been a privilege to work alongside Alan. His compassion for the poor and commitment to give back to those that lost so much has being evident in all the years I've known him. This is his nature and that is what moves his heart for God's people."

Sanna Rajapakse; *Senior Pastor of New Life Church, Colombo, Sri Lanka*

"This is an inspirational book about God's faithfulness and mercy, about a life full of challenges of an amazing man. I met Alan in 2004 and since then he has become a dear friend, a good mentor and an example for me to follow in my own life story. I believe that this book will inspire you, and maybe even become a beacon in difficult times, bringing peace and confidence in the goodness of our Lord."

Irina Trofimova; *Founder and Director of NGOs 'Children of Tien Shan' and 'Path to Victory'. Director of Raising Families, Kyrgyzstan*

"I have had the blessing of a friendship with Alan for over 25 years. His early ventures to Nicaragua brought to us a very consequential stability and vision, with such a perceptive kindness that is outside of the box of most of us. However, until reading this book, I hadn't grasped all that Alan was brought out of, and still to be called into: working with churches in Azerbaijan, Belarus, Ukraine, Kyrgyzstan, Rwanda, Swaziland, Uganda and Zambia. Alan, always learning and sharing, practicing the second commandment, thanks for challenging me, again."

Dr. (Hon) Bob Trolese; *President, Verbo Christian Ministries, Managua, Nicaragua*

"Alan Cutting's 'Cutting Across the Borders', reflects his inspiring life story in a humble way. The book is well written, it brings an account of the ultimate marvellous breakthrough of God's promises, the limitations of man's abilities notwithstanding. Grab the book and read it. You will see the exciting results of faith at work."

The Most Rev. Dr. Onesphore Rwaje; *Retired Archbishop of the Anglican Church of Rwanda*

"Drawing on his extensive travels and life experience, in this inspiring book Alan Cutting recounts story after story of God's faithfulness and provision in the midst of the highs and lows of life. You will laugh, be encouraged, and your faith will be strengthened through seeing the global Church in action through the eyes of a genuine, honest and humble servant of Jesus Christ."

Simon Barrington; *Founder and Director, Forge Leadership Consultancy*

"I have known Alan since 2011, when I became a volunteer with the Samaritan's Purse Disaster Assistance Response Team (DART). In all my interactions with him he has been a man of humility and integrity, with a huge pastoral heart. I am incredibly grateful for the support he has provided me with on my return from overseas DART responses. I would encourage all to read this book and capture Alan's heart for the lost and destitute, and his radical passion to pursue them across nations and continents."

Dr Nathalie MacDermott, BSc MBBCH MRCPCH; *Wellcome Clinical Research Training Fellow, Imperial College London*

"Alan possesses an extraordinary eye for joyfully noticing the tiniest, yet profound indications of the inbreaking Kingdom of God in the most surprising places - places where most see only pain and brokenness. Without minimizing reality, he names and articulates what he sees in a way that the rest of us can begin to notice it too. This is the gift of his story that is most urgently needed for today's cynical and despairing times."

Gordie Lagore MA, GradDipCS (Regent College); *Lead Pastor and Spiritual Director, Vancouver Eastside Vineyard Church*

"This is a deeply personal story. Open, honest, inviting and at times all too painfully raw. But much more, it's a story of God's personal attentiveness to the depths and heights of our human experience, and the discovery of grace and beauty at unexpected moments and in surprising places. If you read with soft eyes you will see your own story of triumphs and setbacks reflected in its pages, and hear for yourself the gentle invitation this book offers to discover that same grace and beauty."

Rev Simon Harris; *Senior Pastor, Burlington Baptist Church, Ipswich*

CUTTING ACROSS THE BORDERS

CUTTING ACROSS THE BORDERS

Alan Cutting

CONTENTS

ACKNOWLEDGEMENTS

had a few permission issues that prevented me from publishing this book until now, but the efforts of Kathy Morrison and Len Pearson in proof reading the original version several years ago have not been forgotten. Thank you.

I also want to thank my current proof reader, Pat Strange, my editor, who wished to remain anonymous, and my self-publishing technical advisor, Kamal Mamedov. Your support and corrections, challenge and suggestions have been so helpful. Thank you.

I also appreciate the endorsements of my esteemed friends and colleagues, and am honoured to have lived life alongside you in so many wonderful and diverse parts of the world. Thank you.

There are so many great people who I have walked with over the years, and could have so easily featured in this life story. But I have tended to resist mentioning too many of you by name, and I have changed the names of some of those I have mentioned. However, for those of you who know that you have played a significant part in forming and shaping my life, and yet haven't been mentioned, well, you know you will get your recognition and reward in heaven. But I also hope that here on earth, I have been faithful in personally voicing my appreciation of you over the years. Thank you.

Finally, and with all my heart, I thank you Bela for being my one flesh, my better half, my best friend and my rescue package. Your prayer and support while I've sought get my brain around this project has been magnificent, patient, long-suffering, stirring and encouraging. Thank you.

INTRODUCTION

applied for my first passport later than most of my peers; in fact, I was almost 30. Having now visited more than 95 countries and territories, I can distinctly recall a couple of childhood memories that, unbeknown to me at the time, were later to become very significant in my life's travels.

One such memory is of a Christmas present I received in about 1963: a Philip's Practical Atlas published in 1961. I still have it. Inside the front cover, in childlike handwriting, are written the words 'Alan Cutting, 43 Pine View Road, Ipswich'. I would turn to pages 24-28 and stare at the incredibly long, mysterious, unpronounceable names of towns and cities in the Soviet Union and think: "This might as well be the *moon*." Here was a totally different and inaccessible world: the enemy (or so the BBC told us) whose collective power-crazed finger hovered constantly over the button marked 'Bomb'.

These days with my second wife, who is from Azerbaijan, and my many very close friends from all over the former Soviet Union, we laugh at the dichotomous impressions we had of each other from those days when, under Khrushchev and Brezhnev, *perestroika* was unimaginable.

And I have another travel-related memory from my childhood: this one involves a dream. Having clearly become a Christian when I was eight years old, it wasn't very long - probably a year or two - before I began to day-dream repeatedly about going to far-away lands and telling people about Jesus. The dream always involved me speaking from a stage, or a platform. I would have this dream so regularly that the images, even the details, became well established in my mind's eye. Then my unassuming reason would come guiltily to its senses, and I would apologise. "I'm sorry, Lord," I would say. "I'm dreaming dreams that are far too big for me. I'm just your servant." And with that I would bashfully push away the dream, until it would stir up inside me on another day.

In recent years I have told this story to people in many nations and cultures all over the world, and I conclude by telling my audience that God actually responded to the *dream* rather than to the apology.

In 2009 I told this story in Atiak, a small rural town in Northern Uganda. I was leading a team of UK volunteers that had journeyed there to learn about the water and sanitation programmes that were supported by my employer, Samaritan's Purse. We visited the Connect Africa Resource Centres (CARC) in Northern Uganda, one of which is situated in the mainly Acholi village of Atiak, just twenty kilometres south of the South Sudanese border. Atiak is a small town made world famous by two massacres, one in 1995 and another a decade later, when the Lord's Resistance Army (LRA) attacked and killed an unknown number of its adults and children. Local people told us, "They showed no mercy. They torched the houses, raped and butchered." We heard stories of how children had been rounded up, forced to eat the chopped up remains of their headmaster, before being killed, and the parents told that if they took the bodies for burial, they too would be murdered. Consequently the rotting remains of their children lay down the road at the school for months.

Ours was a team of twelve. The ten guys slept on cots in one room, the two women were in a separate room, and many of the locals slept in other corners of the primitive CARC centre. Though the shooting stars were magnificent, they didn't light the path to the eco-san toilets, which were quite a trek away, at the back of the centre.

Connect Africa work through the local pastors and churches to encourage a holistic style of ministry (or service) into each community in which they have a presence. Simple clean water and sanitation technology are as much a part of their Christian witness as preaching, teaching and healing the sick. All these aspects of the Kingdom of God nestle comfortably alongside one another in their work, without conflict or debate.

So that night, Wednesday 17 June 2009, as part of their offering to the village, 'Connect Africa' hosted one of their occasional three-night festivals on the town's tufted football pitch, bordered not by terracing, floodlights or changing rooms but by tiny round huts made of straw roofs and cow-dung walls – the dwelling place of thousands of Internally Displaced People.

An area the size of a five-a-side pitch was roped off in front of the stage, which unfolded out of an old truck – PA, speakers, lights and all. The local believers were invited inside the ropes, where they spent two hours worshipping, dancing and, let's be honest, gathering a crowd. That night the crowd attracted by their worship reportedly numbered around 3,000. Unexpectedly, it was then that the CARC director quite casually asked us foreigners to lead the evening's festivities - just because we were there.

My team looked at me wide-eyed. Just before leaving the UK, one by one, they had talked openly and vulnerably with one another about the heavy blows life had recently dealt them. They had shared about how tender they were feeling at this particular time in their lives, even to the point of being unsure as to whether they should come on the trip or not. They had confessed how much they lacked confidence, even over the relatively simple practical task of the team which was, ostensibly, merely to observe the water and sanitation programmes to which Samaritan's Purse was committed in Uganda. And here I was, giving them about 15 minutes' preparation to lead a whole evening of power evangelism in front of an audience of 3,000 traumatised people, not one of whom spoke English.

Carl had a guitar (which he had brought on the trip for team devotionals) and I knew that Tom used to preach. "Well, guys," I asked, "are you up for it?" Carl was happy to lead worship, but Tom said no to preaching. "I'm sorry, mate," he said with the strain of defeat all over his face. "You know I used to do that sort of thing but, since my wife was unfaithful and left me, life has fallen apart for me. I left all that sort of ministry thing behind years ago. That's why I've just got my head down making money these days. Sorry mate, but I just can't help you tonight."

Now I'm not a pushy guy, and 99% of the time I would have accepted that answer without question. And yet that evening something prompted me to ask again. Again Tom said no. So I said, "OK Tom, no worries. But after Carl has done his stuff, I'm going to tell a story, and then I'm going to turn to you where you're standing in the shadows on the edge of the stage, and I'll simply ask you: 'Tom, yes; or Tom, no?' If you say yes, the stage is yours. If you say no, I carry on preaching, and no one will have any idea what that snippet of conversation was about." In response, Tom just had the time to shrug his shoulders at me and, with interpreter in tow, we were hustled into position. It was time to start.

So I got Carl to belt out some songs – 'Greatest Day in History/O Happy Day' (huge cheer) - we told our audience where we were from (Liverpool, Manchester; two more huge cheers and big stirring of intrigue in the crowd), and then I told them all a story.

What was the story I told to these 3,000 impossibly pained people of Atiak that evening? Well, as the crowd spilled out of their little mud and straw huts, and pressed in to cover the length and breadth of the football pitch and beyond, and a stormy darkness fell over yet another day of abject and lethargic poverty, with all my heart I wanted this unbelievably battered community to dare to dream dreams again. So I simply told them the story of my guilt-ridden and repeated childhood dream - the one about me crossing cultures and standing on a stage to share the love of Jesus with crowds of people - and of how as a lad I kept repenting, and of how God had heard the *dream*, not the apology.

And as I testified, and as I looked down onto that frail portable stage and out into the swollen crowd, slowly an incredible, spine-shivering realisation dawned on me. I'd been here before! It was *here*! This was it; this was absolutely it. This was the stage. This was the crowd. This was the setting. This was the event. This was the very place I used to see in my dreams in 1963! I had actually seen Atiak, Northern Uganda, and this rickety little platform, 46 years previously. Amazing.

But I had no time to get too emotional about this extraordinary and supernatural revelation. After all, there were 3,000 people staring at me and waiting for the rest of the meeting. So, finishing my story, I turned my gaze to the edge of the stage and, in a quiet voice simply asked, "Tom, yes; or Tom, no?"

"Yes!" said Tom, and jumped forward to take the microphone from me. Loving nothing better than to help equip and restore people, especially those who have felt defeated by disappointments, I was *delighted*. And do you know what? I don't think I have *ever* heard anyone preach as powerfully as Tom did that night in Atiak. Hundreds of people asked to receive Christ that evening. Many were healed, and delivered from ugly demons that manifest themselves through the writhing of bodies on the ground.

My team, the vast majority of whom had never previously witnessed demonic manifestations or been involved in deliverance (certainly not in the way they were happening that night), just had to get on with it. Whatever conclusions their carefully-analysed theological viewpoints might have led them to believe up till that point in their lives, they knew that there, writhing and screaming before them, was a massive spiritual need and, right there and then, it was going to have to be Jesus or bust.

The training I gave my team on deliverance ministry that night was restricted to one-line instructions yelled into team members' ears over the commotion as they laid hands on people and prayed. So ugly was the manifestation of one of the demons that one team member physically took a large step backwards in shock, almost landing on my foot. I pushed him forward again, shouting to him above the din, "Ian, if ever you believed in the Name of Jesus, then believe in it now!" And in he went again for more.

It was an open heaven. Quite extraordinary!

After the main event, the evening was scheduled to end quite late with a showing of The Jesus Film. (We were told that sometimes in this setting whole families would stay on till four in the morning watching film after film.) That night a huge rain-storm ended the film show early, and the track back to the CARC centre with its eco-san toilet was paved with puddles. I walked home slowly with Tom, a small torch guiding our way through the pitch black to the concrete floor which was to be our bed for the night. We were almost silent. I remember saying only one thing. "Tom; well done mate. That took a different sort of faith than you needed for the preaching you used to do when you were young, didn't it?" Tom didn't say a word - just shrugged once more, and nodded in almost rueful agreement. He knew exactly what I meant. And another man was on the road to restoration.

The following morning an extraordinarily vivid rainbow arced over the horizon, its ends pressed down into fields of sodden maize. It surrounded us; it dwarfed us; it mesmerised us. It seemed that this particular rainbow just would not fade. We packed our vehicle and left the village and, as the bus carefully dipped and splashed its way through deep red puddles of African mud, I stared quietly out of the window. How did the miraculous events of last night actually happen? My repeated boyhood dream had, quite literally and specifically, been played out before my eyes, with 3,000 people looking on. Why now? Why here? Yet again I was forced to reflect on the overwhelming faithfulness and spectacular promises of God and how, despite my limited abilities, my questionable confidence and the sheer harmlessness and normality of my life, He had steered me to so many amazing places, introduced me to such extraordinary people, and done such magnificent things for me. Whatever the boundaries, borders and limits I had set up for myself, God had pushed me through them all.

So I present to you my story so far. It leads you through my nervous but rescued childhood. It opens a door into the intensive community lifestyle that I lived in my twenties and thirties. And it tussles with the pain, betrayal and disasters that I encountered during my forties.

And the rest is geography. I invite you to journey with me on the relentless, unusual and often extreme global adventures of my fifties and sixties. It's a story of people, of places and of relationships; a true and radical tale of love and passion, of vulnerability, determination and betrayal, of rescue and grace, hope and faithfulness.

And although it's a testimony full of facts, I trust that leaking out through most of its pages you will find values, purpose, calling, journey, mystery and grace.

CHAPTER ONE
SUFFOLK CHILDHOOD

For the first six years of my life I lived in Earl Soham, Suffolk, with my father, mother and older sister Kathy. Well, I say *in* Earl Soham - it was actually a couple of miles down a tiny gap between the village church and a thatched cottage; half lane, half stream - the back road to Framlingham and Kettleburgh. Not the end of the earth, it's true, but it did share the same post code. From this 600-year-old house, Dial Cottage - frighteningly haunted, with low ceilings, horrible green mould up the walls, and with no toilet, water, gas or electricity - on tiptoes, and when the corn had not grown to its full height, across the fields I could see the historic Saxtead Green Post Mill.

Frighteningly haunted? Well, for example, early one morning when my father got up, he recalled seeing a classic ghost figure rising up through the ancient spiral staircase. Another time, when my mother was anxious for me when I was sick, she elected to sleep overnight in a normally unused room at the end of my bedroom, in order to keep an eye on me. The room had a noticeably sloping floor. It was such a creepy room; I hated it and wouldn't go into it alone. Several years after we left that house my mother told me what happened that night. During the night she woke up and was mystified to find the window on the wrong wall of the room. She assumed that it was the reflection of car lights playing tricks with her, but fully waking up and investigating some more, she realised there were no car lights, no reflections. A shiver crawled down her spine. The window was actually on the opposite wall from where it should have been. Terrified, she buried her head under the pillow and waited for morning. I was a young adult before I could sleep peacefully in an unfamiliar bedroom.

My father and his brother worked on their father's - my grandfather's - farm, but after my Dad badly injured his back lifting a large sack of peas, the house was sold for £250 and we moved to Felixstowe. I was six.

- - - - -

There in Felixstowe, where he worked for an insurance company, my father's life fell apart. Depressed, on drugs, and having more than one affair, he developed a dreadfully debilitating stammer, and was eventually sectioned to a psychiatric hospital in Belmont, Surrey. During the weekdays my mother, a physically frail but incredibly resilient Aberdonian, would keep this vulnerable little family going, working part-time as an English teacher, and at weekends my father would come home to visit.

I loved and hated weekends all at the same time. I longed for the family to be together and complete, but I couldn't begin to cope with the wild swing of emotions and the inexplicably tense atmosphere when my father came home. The theme music of 'Dixon of Dock Green' - a drama series that was on television at the time - can still make me weep. I associate it with those weekends.

Once when Mum was teaching, and I was waiting on the front door step of the house for her and my sister to return home, a young man who lived nearby invited me to his house to see his collection of model cars. As I went into his bedroom, he shut and locked the door behind me and, although I fought as hard as I could to escape, he wouldn't let me go until he had undressed me and explored me in great detail. Sworn to secrecy, and terrified, I was eventually released and I returned home. I said nothing. I didn't want to add to Mum's burdens, and anyway, I felt ashamed. It was *so* embarrassing. This experience did nothing for my already shaken confidence, and for many years I hated changing-rooms or being trapped or locked in anywhere. Throughout school I remained relatively shy and fearful, didn't make a fuss, and stayed in the background. In fact, I hardly remember the names of anyone I went to school with, and I doubt very much that many would remember me.

I do remember my father had a passion for sharing his weekends not only with his family, but also for inviting children from the local Dr Barnardo's home at Harland House to Sunday tea. I knew these boys and girls from school, and they were trouble. I was heartbroken one Sunday night to find that not only had Dad returned to hospital, but that my favourite model cars, which I kept in pristine condition, had also disappeared. The next day I saw them, scratched and broken, being raced around the tarmac playground.

With increasing regularity, Jehovah's Witnesses would knock on our door. Sensing my mother's vulnerability, they tried to persuade her to join their sect. With at least some nominal 'God awareness' in her past, and in considerable turmoil, she decided to visit the local Anglican vicar, who, I remember to this day, just *radiated* the love and joy of the Lord. He led her to the cross of Jesus and to a real, rescued, redeemed relationship with the Son of God. I was eight at the time.

One weekend a few months later our family was invited to attend an event at Felixstowe Spa Pavilion – a big Christian crusade that was something like a mini Billy Graham festival, and where local band 'Messengers of the Cross' were performing at what must have been one of their very early gigs. I remember where we sat, near the back, central block but on the right-hand side. I don't recall what was said, but I knew I wanted a relationship with Jesus like the one that I could so clearly see had transformed my mother. So when an appeal was made for those who wanted to receive Christ, I asked my Dad, who had been dragged along for the evening, to come with me to the front of the auditorium.

Whether he swore, folded his arms and pretended not to hear me, or just sat there embarrassed I cannot remember, but I went forward anyway. Just as I was, without one plea; or one parent for that matter. I recall the slightly bewildered counsellor, who presumably was all trained up to talk and pray with responding adults. Well, that evening he must have drawn the short straw, and was assigned to talk with me. I'm not sure what he said, if anything, but I do recall him tousling my hair, giving me a booklet to read, and sending me back to my parents!

Such lame counselling could have been a disappointment and anti-climax to me, but it wasn't at all, because *God's* work had been done! I *know*. I know without a shadow of doubt that I repented and accepted Jesus Christ that night, and that His Holy Spirit came into my heart. I was saved, rescued from my sin, forgiven for my *sins*, and have been a grateful Christian ever since.

Twenty-two years later, in 1982, I had an amazing opportunity to look back and reflect on the way God impacted the whole of my family through that day of salvation in my Felixstowe childhood. I had just turned 30, and had been invited to lead worship and speak at a pastors' conference in New Delhi, India. It was my first trip outside of Western Europe, and one afternoon, feeling a little overwhelmed and missing my family, I called into a Christian bookshop that someone recommended that I visit. I picked up a copy of Michael Green's book 'New Life, New Lifestyle' and it opened at Chapter Seven, where the esteemed author quoted the story of a man I knew so well.

> When I was in my early thirties, I became involved with another woman. I fell deep into sin – sin of the ugliest kind – which made me reject all thoughts of God and which very nearly broke up our family life. Five months in a neurosis hospital under the care of some of the finest psychiatrists made no difference to my attitude to life. I came out of hospital worse than when I went in. I had developed a terrible stammer; I took drugs at night to try to help me sleep; I took pep pills during the day to try to keep me going; I went out of my way to avoid contact with anyone at all; I fainted in the streets and I jeered at anyone who tried to help me. I was determined to carry on with my selfish and sinful way of life, no matter what hurt it caused other people.

> Then one Christmas, my son Alan (who was then just eight years old) gave me a picture of the Lord Jesus standing at the door knocking. "Behold, I stand at the door and knock; if anyone hears my voice and opens the door, I will come in to him and eat with him, and he with me." (Revelation 3:20.) For a long time I deliberately turned away from that picture. But the knocking became more and more insistent until finally, at 10.00pm on the 26th June, 1961, in utter desperation and almost unbelief, I said, "Lord, you say you can change people's lives – come into my heart and change mine." At last I had taken that step of faith, and immediately my prayer was answered. There was a complete transformation in my life from that moment onwards.

Michael Green 'New Life, New Lifestyle', p111-112, Hodder and Stoughton, 1973

To get away from the pain (and the illicit relationships) of Dad's past, it was almost inevitable that our family had to move. But I will forever give my Father and Mother (who died in 1985 and 1992 respectively) great honour and respect for demonstrating to Kathy and me just how all-important, how radical a decision it is to follow Jesus, by selling up and moving to Ipswich.

There I completed junior school, failing my eleven-plus exams and quietly stumbling through secondary school. If pressed I could recollect the names of one teacher and five other students from those five years of my life. Feelings of inadequacy drove me to a simple policy: Just keep your head down and don't make a fuss.

The one happy recollection I have concerns cross-country running. But even in this sport that I loved and was good at, I would only come second, week after week. Sadly for me there was a national champion runner in my class, tempting my insecure teenage mind to conclude that even that which I was good at would still only result in being second best. However, one day the champion decided to mess around at the back of the pack. My moment of glory, I thought. But another boy beat me that day, and once more I finished in second place.

Outside of school, my early teenage interests morphed from knowing the details of every car and number plate that ever graced our roads; to cycling; to playing and watching football. By the time I was twelve, I would regularly cycle 100 miles in a day (120 miles was my record), on my own, on an old bike with three gears and dubious metal rod brakes. When I was fourteen I personally organised every detail of a week's holiday which involved me and a friend cycling from Ipswich to the Peak District and back, staying at Youth Hostels each night. Characteristics of resilience, determination and endurance, together with an ability to organise, were slowly forming within me.

But watching football was to be my lasting hobby. I blame my father! He took me to my first Ipswich Town game in 1962, a month before they won the First Division championship. It was a 1-0 win over Cardiff City. He took me to my first away match, a 0-4 defeat at Charlton Athletic, in 1966. Against their better judgement, he persuaded my school and then the Civic College I attended that it was of great educational value to give me time off to attend evening away matches.

Within three years I was attending every game, home and away. This would sometimes involve leaving Ipswich at midnight on a Friday night in order to arrive at Newcastle, Stoke, Huddersfield, Blackpool, or wherever, in good time for the match.

It had become no longer a matter of asking 'What shall we do this weekend?' but 'Let's look at the fixture list to see where we'll be this weekend'. It wasn't until

1973, having watched hundreds of consecutive home games and hundreds more away games that God spoke deeply to me about my obsession (deeply enough for me to listen, that is), and in response I willed myself to deliberately miss a home game. Just one game and it was broken. No longer was my diary planned around the fixture list. I was free to pick and choose.

So, in jest, I blame my father. However, my father blamed *his* father. My grandfather was seriously gassed in WW1 when serving with the 4th Battalion The King's Liverpool Regiment in France in 1915, and lived until his death – which was on my twelfth birthday in 1964 – with a grotesque cough that I thought would kill him every time I heard it. He was a lawyer working for Gotelee and Goldsmith in Ipswich, and was the Ipswich Town FC solicitor from right back in their amateur days through to when they won the First Division and then beat AC Milan in the European Cup. I grew up on stories of how it was he who chose the team's blue and white colours, and of the day when FIFA President, Sir Stanley Rouse, came to dinner. His signature remains to this day on the original share certificates issued by the club. I remember how he occasionally used to take me to watch a match in the directors' box, including the notoriously famous match in 1964 when Sheffield Wednesday players fixed the game for a bet. Albeit, usually over fish and chips in the dubious shadow of some murky stadium somewhere, I've dined out on such prestigious history for years.

Feeling some pressure to develop late (this was the hope and encouragement I regularly received from my parents, who were desperate to say *something* educationally nice when comparing me with my sister, who obviously *had* developed early), I signed up for but utterly wasted two more years at the local Civic College. This time, I remember the names of *no* teachers and *no* fellow students. I just vaguely remember riding around town on the back of someone's motor scooter when I should have been in class. Oh the dreadful, hopeless lethargy of forcing myself to attend college for two whole years, only to fail my 'O' levels; *and* fail the resits; *and* fail the architecture technician exams that I tried next, whilst working for a local architect for 18 months on £5 per week (in fact for the first two weeks probation period I was paid £2 per week)! I would be in my fifties before I would next attempt any formal education.

It was whilst working for the architect that my parents broke some big news. It was one of those "Sit down, son; your mother and I have something to tell you" sort of moments. Basically, it was to be a typical parent/teenager conversation, only the other way round. It went more or less like this. "Now that you are seventeen, Alan, *we* are leaving home".

I was actually delighted for them. My sister Kathy was about to be married, and Dad had been accepted as a mature student to train to become a Church of England clergyman at Ridley Hall, Cambridge. Having passionately lived for Christ since his radical repentance and conversion nine years previously, he longed to spend his whole life serving the Lord, and this was the door that opened up for him.

Up till then Kathy and I had attended the twin Anglican Churches of St Lawrence and St Stephen in the centre of Ipswich that had become our parents' spiritual home. The weekly church services of St Lawrence (which houses the oldest circle of church bells in the world), and St Stephen (which is now home to the Ipswich Tourist Information Centre) were dreadfully dull for teenagers. However, the levels of excitement and drama in the youth club that Dad ran more than made up for it. Through this club he created a haven of acceptance for many young people, as well as the not so young, including alcoholics, drug users, and every sort of dysfunctionality that could stagger into the church hall in St Stephen's Lane. Quite a number came to Christ, and this initiative opened the door for a thriving youth work that blossomed in the town centre during the 60s and 70s. Although I was always the shy one in the background, seeing God at work in such amazing ways did a lot to keep me on track during those teenage years.

So my parents moved to Cambridge, where Dad successfully trained, and served as a Curate at St Martin's Church in Cambridge and as a Rector of the village parishes of Bury and Wistow (near Ramsey, Cambridgeshire) before his ill-health, early retirement and death from cancer at the age of 60. In fact, the eldest Cutting son for four generations died either of cancer or of cancer-related diseases, and 60 was their average age.

At my mother's home on the afternoon of my father's funeral, while we were entertaining the guests who had attended, there came a knock at the door. It was the doctor, who had arrived with the results of my mother's recent blood tests which confirmed that she too had cancer. She lived another seven years before dying in 1992. Sadly, I missed her funeral by being in a Nicaraguan jungle at the time of her death.

But I'm racing ahead of myself. When my parents moved to Cambridge, I moved a mile or two up the road and lodged with Mrs Moore, a delightful elderly widow who treated me like her own son. Somehow I blossomed during that time. It was not just the fact of having a car and a new-found liberty, but somehow I shed most of my fears and inhibitions, and realised just how much I enjoyed responsibility and leadership.

I joined a youth group and soon found myself leading it. Since then, wherever I've worked, and whatever my job description, to this day I describe myself as a pastor, who started pastoring when 18 years of age. God started answering *my* prayers (not just those of my parents). I found a hunger for life, for reading the Bible, and for serving the poor. And there were girls in this fledgling church - *real* girls. Girls you could be friends with, rather than girls you had to impress. What blessed relief!

During this time I recall regularly praying for the guy who had locked me into his bedroom against my will when I was a child in Felixstowe. I found that I now felt sadness for him, and although I had not seen or heard of him since moving to Ipswich, I specifically asked God for the opportunity of meeting him and expressing forgiveness to him. When a fringe member of the youth group said she was planning to bring her new boyfriend to a meeting, I thought nothing of it, but as soon as I saw him and he saw me, neither of us were in any doubt that we had met before. I talked to him calmly about our being neighbours in Felixstowe, looking clearly into his eyes with peace and confidence, and expressing the warmest of welcomes to him. What God did in him I have no idea, and I never saw him again, but for me this was a wonderful answer to prayer, and an occasion when I could see for myself just how powerful and liberating forgiveness can be.

There was another group in town at that time, learning alongside us what it was to be a young house church. The leaders of this group were older and had much more experience than we did. And they had received the Baptism in the Holy Spirit. We would join with them from time to time, and through these meetings I met my first wife. She jumped ship and came to our little house church, but still persuaded me to seek more of the Holy Spirit in my life.

This was a big issue for me. I loved God, He was clearly at work in me, but I could see from the lives of many of those who claimed to have received the Baptism in the Holy Spirit that there was much I was missing. I so clearly remember the week that a mission team called 'In the Name of Jesus' rode into town. After they had ridden in, one of their vehicles broke down. Having been much more familiar with a repair strategy that involved lifting the bonnet and tinkering with the engine, I was taken aback that this group merely laid hands on the bonnet of the van, and the thing burst into life! So many amazing things happened that week. I saw more miracles than I'd seen in my whole life. Night after night people were receiving

Christ, being baptised, healed, and Baptised in the Holy Spirit. People were praying in tongues and being delivered from demons.

Of course I argued on the basis of theology, but slowly as the week went by I was becoming more real with myself. This wasn't honestly a theological issue for me at all. It was an emotional one. Flawed characteristics though they are, being in control and being proud are massively important for the English (and probably for many other cultures around the world as well). But for some reason or another, God doesn't seem to make many concessions for either pride or our need to be in control, and eventually, on the final night of the mission, I asked the team leaders, Clive Calver and Graham Kendrick, to pray with me for the Baptism in the Holy Spirit.

It was the letting go that I found impossibly difficult. I tried hard to let go, but trying hard and letting go are actually activities that pull in opposite directions. One is based on effort and the other on grace. The harder I tried, the more intense I became. At one point I remember saying, "it's all of you now God, and none of me". Except it wasn't! It was still all of me, trying hard to copy all of God. I went home embarrassed and confused. I was disappointed with myself, and the temptation to slink back into my old comfort zones was very real. And what's more, the mission ended that night and the team drove out of town in their miraculously healed van.

A week later, and emotionally things had settled down a bit for me. With our fledgling church, I attended a youth service in Walton, Felixstowe. It wasn't a particularly outstanding time of worship, but at one point during it, the overwhelming love of God just poured over me, again and again and again, and I experienced His *presence* like never before. This has always reminded me of Jesus' friend Thomas (John 20:24-29), and his need to *see* in order to believe. This was God's moment for me - the day it rained in colours in Greytown - the moment when Jesus 'came and stood among them', and when my relationship with God was transformed from one dimensional to three dimensional.

Life changed rapidly after that. We were married in October 1974, and about three or four months after that I took my wife to meet a couple I knew, who had moved to Northamptonshire. They were originally from Ipswich, and were one of the couples that my father had helped develop in their lives in Christ as teenagers. They had subsequently completed Bible College, and had been invited to pastor a small Baptist Church in Thrapston, Northants. We had heard that God was at work there in an interesting way.

We spent a weekend with Dan and Lyn, and their new extended household. We shared our vision for local church, and they shared theirs. There were so many similarities, so many coincidences, and we sensed that something special was happening. They shared with us their dream for having another couple to come and work with them in the church, and we dared to talk practically about what that could mean. At the end of the weekend, we didn't want to come home. Although in those single-carriageway days it could take three hours to drive the journey, we agreed to stay over the Sunday night and leave very early for work in Ipswich the next day. Over a hasty breakfast the following morning Dan merely asked us: "Well, are you coming?" And we simply replied "Yes". We were 22 and 20 years old, and our lives were simply about to begin.

CHAPTER TWO

THRAPSTON

Although Thrapston Baptist Church had been at the centre of the William Carey modern missionary movement in the late 18th century, by the 1970s it was struggling to survive, attended by a few elderly people and with precious little vision for itself, let alone for its community.

But in 1972 the church had invited as their new pastors Dan and Lyn, a young couple straight out of Spurgeon's Bible College, and things rapidly changed over the next couple of years. We were invited to join them as assistant pastors in April 1975, and were given the use of a three-bedroom semi-detached house that had been recently vacated by another couple in the church.

Everyone in evangelical and charismatic churches in those days seemed very impressed by the expression 'full-time worker', and at the tender age of 23 years and one month, I was going to become an FTW. But the reality of what that meant was a big jolt to my system.

The morning after our exhausting move from Ipswich to Thrapston, the alarm went off at 5.20am. The leadership team met to pray three mornings a week at six o'clock. I remember how shocked I was at this level of commitment, but tried to give the impression that I was well used to such early morning activity. These guys clearly took things seriously, and in my heart of hearts, it made me feel like I'd simply been playing a few part-time Christian games in comparison.

A couple of acutely embarrassing experiences in my first few days in Thrapston challenged my confidence seriously. One was being asked to speak at the local secondary school assembly, and being marched into the school hall and onto the stage at the final moment before I was due to speak. As I turned round, I had my first glimpse of a large hall full of cynical teenagers only a few years younger than I was; slouched low in chairs, arms folded, and chewing gum. It was terrifying. Having been built up as the new sensation to hit town, I proceeded to stumble through a few introductory sentences before drying up completely. It was so painful. The kids loved it, and refused to let me forget my debut performance for a long time. And the town was much too small for me to hide away.

Alarmingly sobered by the limited ability of his new staff member to communicate in public, Dan sought some way to build up my confidence. Maybe something practical would help. So the following week he and I agreed to offer our services to a harassed and anxious farmer (and church member) for a day, to help him out after he'd got seriously behind schedule with harrowing his land. We spent a great day on a couple of tractors, and did a really worthwhile job on the fields. I had a satisfying glow of contentment and fulfilment as Dan led our convoy of two tractors back to the farm sheds. That was until Dan, for some reason, stopped his tractor dead in its tracks. And I didn't. Suddenly there was a bang. (Now I must be honest; I'm never really sure why people use that expression – after all, it's not often that *gradually* there is a bang.) The benefit of our contribution to the farmer was lost in one second, as boiling water hissed menacingly out of my tractor's radiator. Pete the farmer was not grateful, and left the church soon after this unfortunate event. Whether or not his departure was connected in any way to my limited manoeuvring skills with his expensive agricultural machinery, I never found out.

Other painful events followed, but somehow God used each of them, little by little, to help me deal with failure and embarrassment, and to become a learner, a servant, a follower and a leader.

My wife and I had previously lived in a horrid little damp flat on Norwich Road in Ipswich, so the house we were given upon arriving in Thrapston was amazing. We planted vegetables in the garden, invited old friends from Ipswich to come and stay, and tried to come to terms with our new life. But we hardly settled, and never ate the vegetables, because within four months we'd moved again, this time into the recently formed Shekinah Community household. We were now one of three couples living together with young children and one previously homeless single girl.

What do I mean by Shekinah Community? Well, as a young church, we had become totally intrigued with the lifestyle of the first Christian disciples (as outlined in Acts 2:42-47), and again and again we found ourselves asking one question. Could what we called an Acts 2 lifestyle still work today? Would it be feasible to live just like the early believers did? And if we did, would we see the same blessing, favour, miracles and growth as they did? We were determined to find out, and so, for a number of years in the 1970s and 80s, we attempted to devote ourselves to the same way of life those early believers were devoted to, and to model our lives on the lifestyle and practices that we read about in that passage of scripture. To make this a reality, many of us lived together in what we called a common-purse community, and this community was at the very core of our life as a church.

But however shocking it had seemed to me to wake at 5.20 am to pray, it wasn't until we moved into that shared household that the reality of what it meant to follow Christ *really* hit me. For several months, and with my life forcibly rubbing so closely against the lives of others, I struggled deeply with my own selfishness, and felt that I had backslidden into being a proud, self-consumed, irritable, withdrawn young man, trapped in a lifestyle that I couldn't cope with and couldn't see a way out of.

But gradually over that winter I came to terms with the intensity of this shared lifestyle, grew to like it, then to love it and believe in it, and gained confidence again as a broken, cleansed and transformed man of God.

By April 1976, the month our first son was born, we were a household of 17 people living energetically for Christ in a four-bedroom house (the Baptist Manse).

Every community has a focus, or a purpose. People tend to live together either by necessity (for economic reasons, or due to imprisonment, etc), or to fulfil a task (oil rig workers, Bible College students, etc), or to make a point (hippies, ecologists etc). Our focus was simply a desire to follow God; to practise the presence of Jesus; to express the values that we felt God wanted to see in every local church. Shekinah – the name we gave to the community - means "the visible manifestation of the radiance, glory or presence of God dwelling in the midst of His people".

Most people tended to describe us as living in an 'extended household', i.e. a household that consisted of a larger number of people than were in a typical household among our neighbours. But it really was such a fulfilling way of living, and looked so normal when viewed alongside Acts 2 - and the way in which much of the world still lives - that with a twinkle in our eye we sometimes referred to those who *didn't* live this way as living in 'diminished households'.

Only two members of the community household had paid jobs, and two more of us worked for the church. The two of us who worked for the church were each given a £20 per month allowance from the church.

All together we learned what it meant to lay down our lives for one another. Once that meant sending one of our members to Canada just to give a grieving person a hug. Other times it merely meant being prepared to be the first one to be willing to run upstairs to fetch a jumper for someone else.

We explored with ruthless honesty what it meant to die to ourselves and follow Christ. Many times Dan and I stood together publicly and said of one another, "He knows everything there is to know about me" - and it was true.

As the community grew, more and more broken and dysfunctional people were drawn to come and live with us, attracted by the sense of order, security and the overwhelming ambience of love, acceptance and forgiveness. One girl, horrendously abused then totally rejected by her family, had run away and had lived in the sewers of a nearby town before coming to live with us.

An alcoholic man who came to Christ was a compulsive liar and thief. In the frailty of his new life, he would regularly steal money from the household and disappear for days on end on a drinking binge, only to return, often with deep remorse and *occasionally* with real repentance, desperately seeking something between a new start and a hot meal.

Another guy, whilst on drugs in Belgium, had lived for months in a room that he had painted completely - doors, walls, ceiling, floor and windows (including the glass) - with black paint. His excesses had totally wrecked his mind, but he and his wife had come to Christ. A community in North Wales had given him a home for a year, but those who led it were at the end of their tether with him, and asked us if we would take him on. He did well for a couple of years, but one Sunday afternoon he relapsed and, on a high after smoking banana skins (and when all the men from the household had gone for a walk) he found a gun and burst into one of our households, shooting pellets around a room full of women and young children. Thankfully no-one was physically hurt, but that was one of two gun incidents we were involved in with people we were trying to help.

We needed all the people resources we had, and more, to help these people become delivered, healed and stabilised, so even the few household members who *had* been employed decided to leave their places of work. If God had brought these people to us, we reasoned, God would provide for us. If He provided, we would eat. If He didn't, we wouldn't.

We shared a common purse. There wasn't much in it, but we shared it anyway. We were all together and had everything in common (Acts 2:44). We had a head of household (who was Dan, the senior pastor) but we agreed all major decisions together at what we called our daily household time. We met every evening at nine o'clock and had at least an hour when we worshipped, prayed and broke bread. We confessed our sins to one another, learned to share all our fears and failings, prayed and supported and forgave one another.

These painful times of getting right with each other were regularly undertaken in public, as we frequently had several guests staying with us. These were usually but not always believers, either from the rest of the church, or relatives, or others who had heard about us from around the country. Visitors didn't knock on the door. We encouraged them just to come in. Apart from the sanctity of our marriages, the only thing we committed *never* to share with our visitors was our need for money or food, although more often than not this was blatantly obvious.

The way most people joined the community was by visiting it, more and more regularly. So often, we joked, that eventually they just forgot to go home.

It was into this extraordinarily loving yet intense environment that our two sons, Joel and Ben, were born, in 1976 and 1978. Joel was born in Kettering hospital, although I missed the birth due to sickness. It was really more nerves and a sleepless night than sickness, but until I had secured an all clear note from the doctor I was not allowed not visit him.

Partly with this memory, we determined two years later that Ben would be born at home. While the male members of our household played Scrabble downstairs, and the women of the household fussed around, Ben was born in our bedroom. Trying to make me feel good about my role, the midwife suggested I make a fire outside and burn the afterbirth. I dutifully obeyed, but found that I hadn't built a solid enough fire on that damp and windy Saturday night in March, and despite my best efforts to prod and coax, it just would not burn. So I went back indoors to fetch more wood and paper, and returned a couple of minutes later, only to find the placenta had vanished. Where to, I never knew, although I seem to recall a cat slinking away that night with a happy smile on its face.

We saw incredible answers to prayer. Often we had no food. So we ate windfall apples that had fallen from the trees. We made bread with baking powder, plain flour and a touch of margarine and water. One day all we ate was a few dry homemade biscuits. We would come together, hungry, cold, tired, with young babies to care for, and pray. Sometimes people would arrive unexpectedly with food, even as we prayed. Once a local farmer (who wasn't a Christian believer) turned up and said he had grown too much sweet corn for his cattle, and he was about to throw some away. Would we like the sweet corn that his cows couldn't eat?

Or people would come with money. Often tiny amounts of money would be enough for making this simple bread, or to buy a pint of goat's milk for our lactose-intolerant baby. Virtually everything was home-made. It was cheaper that way. We lived incredibly simply, and everything we had spare was either given away or was re-invested back into the development of the church fellowship.

We were given cars. We gave cars away. I've been given houses. I've given a house away.

A fourth couple moved from London to join us, selling their possessions and laying the money at the household's feet. With this capital, by April 1977, we had bought, renovated and moved into what became the second Shekinah Community household, and I was to lead this household. It consisted of our two young families and two more single people.

For a number of years people would regularly encourage me with a scripture from 1 Timothy 4:12 (NIVUK, where the apostle Paul said to young Timothy, "Don't let anyone look down on you because you are young"). As a 25-year-old pastor, father of two, and head of a household of ten, I answered the door once to a salesman who asked me: "Is your mother in?"

Again and again we prayed, and again and again God provided. At least twice we saw *real* miracles, once when a minibus full of visitors arrived unexpectedly, and we wanted to share our last loaf of bread with them. We sliced it, sliced it some more, and continued to slice it. It just didn't get any smaller. And at another time, the same thing happened with a joint of meat. We went quieter and quieter, and our eyes widened, as we realised with awe that we really were on holy ground.

Once we agreed to visit the Christian community household in North Wales that we had struck up a friendship with. Because of the feeding schedules of our babies (Joel was a few months old and the other couple's baby was even younger), we planned to get up at 3.00am in order to leave our home and drive up to North Wales in the early morning. The problem was that at nine o'clock the previous evening we had no money for fuel for the vehicle. We agreed to get up at 3.00am anyway, and go through the motions of leaving, even if we had no money and no fuel. By the time we had woken, through the door of our home over that short night had been placed an envelope, and in it was enough money for the fuel to drive to North Wales. No more and no less. So we went. But when we arrived, apart from us having no money for fuel to drive home, we felt the shame of having nothing to give to our hosts. Our household urgently and discretely prayed about this together over their breakfast table one morning. No-one other than our community members back in Thrapston knew where we were, let alone the address, but as we prayed the post arrived, and among the letters was one addressed to me. In it was cash; enough for us to give a reasonable gift to our hosts, enough for fuel for the return journey, and enough to buy an ice cream in Shrewsbury on the way home.

It was whilst praying for people at a meeting we led at Bedworth Baptist Church that I first experienced people falling over under the power of God. I'd never heard of this happening before, so we were more than a little bewildered by this phenomenon at first. But before long it was happening regularly, and we got into the practice of having people ready to catch those falling.

We also regularly saw people healed. One weekend we invited a man called Ian Andrews to come and speak to the church. Ian had a significant healing ministry, and it was an amazing weekend during which he not only prayed for the sick, but encouraged all of us to do the same. God dramatically healed many people. I recall my favourite example. A four-year-old boy simply prayed for and laid his hands on the ankle of a grandmother who had suffered from severe and lasting back pain, and watched her leg grow at least a couple of inches in his hands, resulting in no more pain. Then the boy just ran off and played with his other four-year-old mates!

The sense of God's presence was extraordinary that weekend. In those days, typically churches might write a cheque for a visiting speaker for about £25. But instead of writing a cheque for Ian from the church that weekend, we invited people to raise what we called a love-offering for him. It came to just over £800.

People ask me still what it feels like to witness a miracle. Well, there is probably a significant percentage of people reading this that have experienced such occurrences. It's wonderful, and a warm shiver goes down your spine as you realise what's happening. But the shiver is not so much about what is physically or practically happening so much as an intense awareness that God the Holy Spirit is manifestly in the very same room as you are. Amazing. But equally, it is also strangely natural - warmly believable rather than incredible and unbelievable. Sometimes the extraordinary and the ordinary walk together; the natural and the supernatural kiss.

We lived that way, communally, intensely, until 1982, when God gradually began to change my focus from an essentially local calling to a church planting and then an international one. In an attempt to delegate some local responsibilities, a slightly-extended household of five of us left our bigger household and went to live in a tiny cottage (with no toilet or bathroom), then seven of us to a semi-detached house, where we stayed for the remainder of our time in Thrapston.

One very special couple that God brought across our path was Gordie and Kathleen Lagore. Having grown up in a very strong and dynamic family who were in high-profile Christian leadership in Canada, the multi-talented and gifted Gordie followed in the footsteps of his prestigious father and uncles, and emerged quickly into public leadership and ministry that spread far beyond the borders of his nation. In 1987, our churches were honoured to host one of Gordie and Kathleen's mission teams, and our hearts were knit together.

So it was with much shock and trauma that we took an international phone call one day, through which we understood that Gordie had just suffered a *complete* nervous breakdown. The pressure of performance-orientated public ministry had quite suddenly taken its toll, done its worst, and a 30-year-old multi-gifted well-known figure had become a shivering wreck.

It was almost impossible for Gordie to recover whilst living in the same environment that had caused the breakdown, and so we invited him and his family to come and live with us in Thrapston. "Just be," we said. "Live, love, walk, sleep, weep, pray and be. The only thing we won't allow you to do is what you have learned to call ministry." Grace-filled permission to be weak, broken and vulnerable was not a gospel that Gordie had had the chance to discover until that point. There had been too many plates to spin, too many people to keep attracting to meetings, too much show to be kept on the road.

The Lagores gladly accepted our offer, and fell into our lives. We gave them our best home - a new detached house recently purchased from the sale of the old Baptist Manse. We gave them a small income and a car, put their children into school, and there they lived, without pressure, and as a loved part of our life together. Kathleen was a magnificent support and resource for Gordie and their children, despite the frightening and uncontrollable change of circumstances that had rocked her family's lives. The time for their annual UK visa renewal came and went. The British government was too busy with the activities of the first Gulf War to bother about renewing or denying recovering Canadians their visas. So they stayed another six months, and during that year and a half, God very gradually put Gordie back together again.

This special friend of mine remains to this day frail, tender, and weeps easily, and no-one can doubt the immense grace and wisdom on the man. Soon after he returned to Canada, he took up the pastorate of the Vancouver Eastside Vineyard Church, which attracts the poorest, most broken, vulnerable people from the notorious Commercial Drive district. One of the weekly tasks the church commits itself to is to wash the feet of the many prostitutes that live around them, following a conviction they had one day that Jesus was asking them to do for these street girls what they had done for Him. It's that sort of church, and Gordie is that sort of man.

I have travelled across the world to lean on his mercy, friendship and wisdom in my own darkest hours.

- - - - -

One practical reason why we opened up the structure of the Shekinah Community was that only about half of those coming to Christ could have ever lived an intense communal life. Others, for example, were married to non-believers. We began to feel that the structure was alienating some of these new believers. Those who couldn't live a shared life were tempted to feel like they weren't quite living the way God was asking them to do. Nevertheless, as the church grew, one-third lived together in some form of common purse community.

We also realised that the intensity of our shared life was alienating many non-believers in the town. Members of the broader community (which tended to either love us or hate us) regularly gossiped about us, and even once generated a front-page newspaper headline strongly criticising us. We didn't want to give the impression that this was the only acceptable model of New Testament Christian living.

So we quietly dismantled the structure of Shekinah Community, and some of its intensity, but most importantly, continued to live by its principles and its values. In this way, we gained evidence which suggested that it became easier for the town, the authorities, and our neighbours to relate to us. We were still oddballs, but not quite as odd as before.

In 1983 my wife and I moved to Kettering, where we took out a mortgage and purchased our own home, but continued to have many families and single people living with us almost constantly for the next decade.

Between 1975 and 1990, we lived with a total of 40 different people. I saw just how deep God could go with lives that were laid at His feet. John 12:24 became the motto verse of our church: "Unless a grain of wheat falls into the earth and dies, it remains by itself alone. But if it dies, it bears much fruit."

- - - - -

So did it work? Did we live like the early believers, and see what they saw? I remain encouraged when putting our experience against what we read in Acts 2:42-47:

	Early church experience (Acts 2)	Shekinah Community experience
v 42	They devoted themselves to the apostles teaching and to fellowship, to the breaking of bread and to prayer	Yes, we learned so much about leadership, loving one another, the presence of God. I've never grown up so much in so short a time
v 43	Everyone was filled with awe and many wonders and signs were performed by the apostles	Yes, there was an incredible sense of awe, and we saw more signs and wonders than I've ever seen before or since
v 44	All the believers were together and had everything in common	Yes
v 45	They sold property and possessions to give to anyone who had need	Yes
v 46	Every day they continued to meet together in the temple courts. They broke bread in their homes, and ate together with glad and sincere hearts, ...	Yes (not in the temple courts, but certainly in our homes)
v 47a	...praising God and enjoying the favour of all the people	Yes (praising God) and yes and no (favour with *some* of the people)
v 47b	And the Lord added daily those who were being saved	No, not daily, but more people came to Christ than in any other church I've been a member of. In 1975, the church consisted of 25 people. In 1990 it numbered 400. That's 1,600% growth, or 25 additional people per year; one every fortnight for 15 years

So from the roots of an intensely *local* calling lasting twenty years, firstly in Thrapston and then in Kettering, God has in the last decade or two given me an intensely *global* calling. *Common* purse gave way to *Samaritan's* Purse. I had no passport until I was in my late twenties, and rarely went anywhere overseas for the next ten years, but have now, according to the official list of the prestigious Travelers' Century Club, visited 96 countries and territories. But I learned the principles of His Kingdom, that now are the bedrock of my value system, in the intensity of close community relationships. They were worked out in openness, confession, forgiveness, walking in the light, holding lightly to possessions and trusting Him to provide.

Have I lost anything by not living this way these days? Well, if required to do so, I could probably justify my present lifestyle in many ways; but in another sense, yes, I've lost a few things. God, as they say, lives at Wits-End Corner, and therefore while we live within the measure of our finances, maintain certain walls of privacy around us and settle for less than a radical walk with God, we are less likely to see miracles and become transformed into His image.

As a young pastor, I was invited to lead worship and teach at a pastors' conference in New Delhi, India, in April 1982. When I told my colleagues I was going, I recall one of them almost falling off his chair laughing, as I had never even eaten a curry in my *life* before. He really thought I wouldn't survive. However, I went, ate my first-ever curry, and got a serious bout of Delhi belly; but with weakness, fear and trembling, and a concave stomach, I still managed to lead worship and to teach. People came from Srinagar in the north to Kerala in the south. It took four days for some of these church leaders to travel to the conference. I'm quite sure the delegates won't remember much about it now, but really it went fine.

But it was what went on in the streets that *really* impacted me. I recall a family - mother, father and two young children - sitting in the gutter at the edge of a busy, dusty city road, listening to a tiny transistor radio and pulling up *weeds* to eat for their lunch. I'd participated in short-term mission teams in Western Europe since 1979. They were cross-cultural, but not like this. The colours, the smells, the chaos, the injustice, the vibrancy, the poverty, the pain, the joy, the fulfilment; the overwhelming sense of fulfilment! When I returned home to the UK I became restless, dissatisfied, demotivated, and at some point each and every day and for the next six months I wept tears. Not just for me, but also for the situations I'd encountered. I was going through a deep sense of loss, a form of bereavement. It was very unsettling, for me and for my family, but as I slowly and painfully worked through these emotions - talking, praying, adjusting values here and making decisions there - this experience was to become completely life-changing.

This was what I call the messiness of God's call on my life. Ever since then I have had a deep burden for the poor, the underprivileged, the marginalised, and have found every opportunity I could, and for decades at my own expense, to come alongside people in forgotten worlds; to walk compassionately with the poor. And as I have done so, I have realised the call to serve God cross-culturally went right back to my childhood.

CHAPTER THREE

KETTERING

As early as 1979 we sent out the original leader, Dan, with his family and a few others, to plant a church in Holloway, North London. The two churches were separated only by distance, and continued to enjoy very close relationship and interaction. Those of us who were left in local church leadership in Northamptonshire grew in experience, and in 1983 it was my turn to be sent out to plant a new church.

As the church in Thrapston grew, it attracted people from the nearby towns of Corby, Kettering, Raunds and Rushden. We would send minibuses and circuit these towns to deliver and return people to our weekend and midweek meetings. We started a home group in Kettering and then, on a leaders' retreat weekend in Felixstowe, God clearly spoke to us all about sending me to plant a church there. This was a big and exciting step and, at age 30, I felt very ready for it.

I'm not sure I'd do it the same way now, because these days I have a greater respect for the church as it already exists in the town, but our strategy was to invite well-known church leaders, healers and Bible teachers to do a very public week-long convention in the town's biggest public hall. Driven either by the enthusiasm of our publicity, or by the Holy Spirit, an encouraging number of people came along. Some were healed and others received Christ. During this time we announced our plans to plant a church, and started meeting on the following Sunday. We arrived on our first Sunday morning to an instant congregation of 50 people. Over the next few months we had a steady flow of people coming and going, until numbers stabilised at around the 60 mark.

Young people, couples, older people and families from all backgrounds came to join us. Many were factory workers, and a number of them could not read or write. We devised what we called a Knowing Jesus Course for new believers, but instead of having manuals, pens and paper for the writing of notes, the KJC format consisted of cartoons, diagrams and doodles, and we scattered coloured crayons around so that the students could colour in the pictures whilst learning about Jesus.

By the beginning of 1985, the church leadership team sensed that God was directing us to buy a derelict warehouse in Alexandra Street. Many years previously this building had functioned as St Luke's Church, and we planned to restore it to its original purpose. With one mind the church members (of whom only about fifteen were wage earners and I doubt if any earned as much as an average wage) set themselves to raise the £25,000 purchase price. This was done in nine weeks, but not before families had sold cars and treasured possessions, adults giving life savings and even children volunteering their pocket money. Not a jumble sale or money-raising event in sight – God told us to believe Him for the money and give till it hurt.

So a derelict warehouse became our base and, with broken windows and the concrete floor covered with puddles from a leaking roof, we gratefully met there whilst renovating it. Within 18 months it had become the comfortable meeting place for the church, able to hold 200 people and incorporating offices for the full-time staff, with a front extension built as a welcoming foyer and extra meeting room.

This was one of three major building schemes I project managed during this era.

As a growing network of churches (for we then planted other churches in Raunds, Corby, Ipswich, Ramsgate, Banbury and Antwerp) we changed our name to Praise Community Church, to reflect our values. Every time we planted a new church we gave our best people away. To one degree or another, each church was painfully birthed out of the womb of the Thrapston mother church. Sometimes she would almost die giving birth, but somehow, again and again, God would attract, nurture and raise up new people, and she would not only survive, but thrive and flourish into child birth once more.

Despite living in different towns and even (in the case of Antwerp) in different countries, we would see and stay with one another very regularly, and the network of Praise Community Churches was extraordinarily strong. Our leadership structure included both local elders and a national leadership team, who were effectively a church-planting unit with responsibility for the oversight of the moral, relational and doctrinal wellbeing of the churches.

Unsurprisingly, as a pastor, from time to time I faced some incredibly difficult pastoral situations. I so clearly recall the young and vulnerable couple who visited us one day with traumatic news. The scan for what was their first baby had revealed that the foetus had a seriously deformed head, and had no chance of living after birth. The hospital had strongly advised an abortion. Through the trauma of the news, this couple were desperate for a miracle, for an answer, for hope. We promised no miracle, but did commit to support them whatever their decision, be it to abort or to continue with the pregnancy. They decided to reject the advice of the hospital, and to continue with the pregnancy, and we walked closely together for the next few months, weeping, praying, listening, loving. It was a painful time. As the time for the birth drew near, we asked them to call us as soon as the mother was admitted to hospital for the birth. The call came at about six o'clock one bright summer Sunday morning. We dashed off to the hospital, and it wasn't until we had parked the car and approached the entrance that my wife reminded me that we had no idea where in the hospital they were. Looking up and instantly pointing to a window, I said: "They are in that room over there." The reason I knew was that standing upright outside one particular ground-floor window was an enormous sentry-like figure, maybe three metres tall, in traditional battle dress and with a staff in his hand. This breathtaking moment was somehow so natural, so comforting. We calmly made our way through the hospital to where the window was and, needless to say, we found our couple in that very room. The baby died at birth, but the awareness of the presence of such a magnificent angel was so reassuring.

In the context of my pastoral duties, I found I was regularly able to lead people to faith in Jesus Christ. It was easy, in the sense that I had the regular opportunity *in public meetings* to bring visitors to the church to the point of decision, and then pray with them, and God did the rest. It was such a joy and privilege to lead people to Christ, and also to baptise them. But outside of that meeting environment, when it came to being an evangelist, I was *useless*! I never knew what to say to *start* a conversation.

Not so with my friend and colleague, Colin, who would regularly give hitch-hikers a lift. As they jumped into his car, he would say, "Do you want to know about the Lord?" and in reply they would cry, "What must I do to be saved?" Or so it seemed to me.

But it didn't appear to work that way for me. They would jump in my car, and I would ask them, "Do you want to know about the Lord?" And they would look at me with a sideways look and reply, "No, of course not. I want a lift."

Determined to crack my evangelistic inability once and for all, I changed my tactics. "Softly, softly," I thought. "Take an interest in them. Ask them a few questions about themselves." So the next time I stopped for a hitch-hiker, he hopped in, we set off down the road and I asked him what he did for a living. He told me he was a student and then asked me, "What about you? What do you do for a living?" Wonderful, I thought. Here comes the opening I've been waiting so long for. Stay calm, Alan. Stay calm. "I'm a pastor," I replied casually. "Really?" he said. "My dad was a plasterer as well." We spent the rest of the journey talking about thistle and finish. I'm not sure I've ever given a lift to a hitch-hiker since.

It's funny, and an aside, but for some reason all my memories of Colin seem to involve cars. For example, early one very icy Saturday morning, three of us were driving along in a very old VW Beetle which we called 'Uffle-sar' (an obscure spin on its registration number, UFL 54) and Colin, who was driving, was deep into telling us a complex story. We turned a corner too quickly and, after the car had spun round 360 degrees, it landed with a heavy bump on the grass verge. Without a moment's pause, Colin continued to tell us his story as though absolutely nothing had happened. In the end we interrupted him. "Colin," I remember saying in a slightly shaky voice. "I think you'll find we've crashed."

I also recall the day that Colin drove along a country road in his estate car, and accidentally ran over a pheasant. "Oh well, that's dinner sorted," he said to himself as he jumped out and slung the remains of the poor creature in the back of the car. However, to Colin's horror, after he had driven another few miles and arrived into the town centre, the bird recovered and continued to flap and squawk around his head until he was able to stop the car safely and let it out.

Yet another time Colin was walking up the road to a home group meeting when a familiar car stopped and parked just in front of him. "That's nice," he thought. "Derek has stopped to give me a lift." He jumped into the back seat of the car, shut the door and, as he fastened the seat belt, he made a pleasant, chatty, if slightly funny greeting. To which the bemused driver, some random bloke delivering pools coupons in the neighbourhood, turned from his driving seat and asked: "Who exactly *are* you?" With acute embarrassment and sincere apology, Colin excused himself, undid the seat belt and fumbled for the door handle in order to make a hasty exit. But the back doors were child-locked. The driver had to get out of his car and walk round to let Colin out.

The church had exceptionally talented musicians and developed various bands for different occasions. These ranged from worship bands to punk bands. They worked locally, across the UK and internationally at worship conventions, music and evangelism concerts, and in schools and clubs.

From our music studio in North London several recordings were made, including one album called 'Songs for Bluefields' which even featured one of my songs. But although I played the guitar and led worship during the 80s in Thrapston and Kettering, the skill and creativity of many of our musicians was light years ahead of mine, and I was delighted to make way for them. I haven't seriously played an instrument for years.

Before Stuart Garrard joined the band Delirious, he worked for Praise Community Churches for a number of years. While living in Kettering, Stuart and I each had a small office next to one another. He would occasionally wander into my office with his guitar round his neck and say, "What do you think of this one?" And he'd strum another of his creations. "Sounds OK to me," I would reply, trying to be encouraging but in reality needing to hear a song several times before I knew whether I liked it or not. These days I still hear those same songs being sung in churches and conferences, in Africa, in Central Asia, in Eastern Europe, in North America and, each time I do, I smile to myself, praise God and remember the song's origins in that little office in the back streets of Kettering.

The spirit of generosity in the church was outstanding. Not only was a huge fund set up for our overseas aid and development work, and not only did the church fund dozens of full-time workers, but informally and without fuss, many people were giving away cars, homes and holidays to one another.

In 1987 a couple we knew, together with their young children, would regularly drive from many miles away to visit our church in Kettering. I guess Martin and Jo were used to long journeys, as they were Australians on a 12-month teacher exchange. They were members of the large and very dynamic Christian City Church in Sydney. They became good friends and, when they returned to their home in the southern hemisphere, they invited us to visit them. Just get yourselves there, they said, and you have a free holiday for a month. Come and receive, and learn from our home church. Dream on, I thought, but didn't say it out loud.

But my wife strongly felt we should go, so we prayed, asking God for the air fares for our family of four to travel to the other side of the world. Sensing that we should commit to an *action* of faith, and despite having just £11 in the bank at the time, we committed to four flights to Sydney, with no get-out clause. We didn't tell a soul what we'd done. That evening I was due to speak at the Thrapston church, and was invited to eat beforehand with our very close friends Peter and Jane. As we ate our meal, Peter told me he had something to discuss with me. God had spoken to them, he said, and they had decided to sell their house, buy a smaller one, and give a lot of money away, including a very generous sum to us. As he outlined what that sum would be, he quoted the exact air fare I had committed to earlier in the day. As I wept over my meal, I told them what we'd done. The house was sold, the money given. We paid for our flights and later were given another surprise gift for our living expenses from a young couple who we were preparing for marriage.

Sydney, and Christian City Church, was altogether enlarging, liberating, faith-building, strategic, and great fun. We spent a month with Martin and Jo and joined in with everything the church was doing. We were also invited to visit Pastor Brian Houston at Hillsong Church. In fact, he drove all the way across the city to pick us up, invite us for tea, take us to his meeting, and drive us home again in the evening. All this on the basis of one brief meeting we had previously had in Birmingham, UK. Hillsong was known in those days (1987) for its *signing* more than its singing – deaf people from all over the city would head there and benefit from the expert signing service which was provided at each church meeting.

We returned to our pastoral duties in Kettering with much enthusiasm. We instantly experienced a new wave of people coming to Christ and, in so many ways, the church pushed forward into new levels of faith and maturity out of that experience. But I recall one very strange meeting with Pastor Dan soon after our return. He was nervous and defensive, and seemed to be panicking over this new-found surge of growth. I remember him strongly warning me: "You know you couldn't do this (leading churches) without me, don't you?" In reply, I remember saying that I didn't actually *want* to do this without him, but that if I did, I could do *some*thing without him, although it might look a bit different. But it was the first disturbing sign of something that eventually was to result in one of the most foundational crises of my life.

In these ways Praise Community Church became established in Kettering. Our numbers continued to grow, week by week, month by month. We quickly became known in town. Our worship band won prizes on the carnival float for its great music, and our street evangelism clowns and jugglers were well known on the shopping street every Saturday morning, as we shared the gospel in a vibrant and colourful way the town hadn't seen before. Despite being a working-class church in a working-class town, within months we had somehow bought a building just off the town centre to use as our church centre, and the local newspaper regularly featured our activities and our opinions.

Like Millwall, not everyone liked us. We were the subject of criticism from people writing to the local press, and others joked about us as that crazy happy-clappy lot who were a bit freaky and embarrassing. Some of our neighbours tried to avoid eye contact or engage in conversation with us.

Then God led us into mission partnerships with churches in Sri Lanka, Romania and Nicaragua. Our hearts became broken by the plight of peoples, nations and churches a lot poorer than our own. Through these church partnerships, we sent doctors and nurses to work in refugee camps in Sri Lanka, we sent project managers to ensure the sustainable development of a medical clinic in Romania, and we raised loads of money and bought land for a farm which enabled the development of education and livelihood opportunities for some of the poorest families in Nicaragua.

As we prayed for our overseas friends and sent people and funds for the support of their work, this led us in turn to see the marginalised people from our *own* town in a new light, and we opened overnight needle exchange facilities for drug users and a second-hand clothing store for people from the local housing estate. We had begun our life as a church with such a burst of energy, noise and colour, seeing the totality of our role in the community as worship, prayer and evangelism, but we were now investing much more of our time and a huge amount of our resources into meeting the needs of the poor, both locally and internationally.

Then I noticed an unplanned spin-off. Gradually I sensed a marked difference in the attitude of the general public towards us. I began to be invited onto community panels and school boards, and people were more comfortable speaking with me on the street, or calling into our church centre just to say "hi" and have a coffee. There was genuine interest in our lives and values. Non-believing strangers donated funds to us for the work we were doing with the poor, and even the local authority offered us grants for some of these initiatives. Where previously people had thought we were credulous, we now had credibility. We'd not stopped worshipping God or declaring the gospel for one moment, but the demonstration of our love for the community and for the poor around the world had changed people's ridicule into respect.

This to me is one of the strongest testimonies of the church I planted in Kettering in the 1980s. More than thirty years on, I still believe that each local church's strategy should be integral: worshipfully connected with its God, lovingly connected with one another, comfortably connected with its community and compassionately and respectfully connected with its world.

God kept stirring a global awareness within our churches until it formed a central aspect of our strategy and existence. While Jesus told us "the poor you will always have with you", there was also a sense that in the UK, the poor were actually quite well catered for. So when we asked God for natural, relational openings into the developing world, through a series of meetings and coincidences those openings were not long in coming. Out of this we formed what we called an Overseas Aid department, which existed to fund and support these sustainable development programmes in Sri Lanka, Romania and Nicaragua.

To Sri Lanka we sent a couple of young doctors from Kettering. Through a relationship we had with Sanna Rajapakse (the pastor of New Life Church in the city of Colombo), the doctors lived and worked there for a year in a Tamil refugee camp. Years later, when employed by Samaritan's Purse, I was to work directly with Pastor Sanna in providing a disaster response immediately following the 2004 Tsunami, although at that stage I had never heard of Samaritan's Purse.

41

To Arad in Romania we sent a white van full of aid, just ten days after the collapse of the infamous Ceausescu regime over Christmas 1989. We followed this up by sending two key couples to Arad for a year, where they waded through the chaos and corruption of early post-communist bureaucracy to oversee the development of a church-run medical clinic which, for many years, and possibly to this day, employed fourteen or so people and provided primary health care with excellence to its community. I made one trip to Romania to visit these couples – little knowing that this would be the first of many, many visits I was to make to Eastern Europe after joining Samaritan's Purse.

But between 1989 and 2003 I would regularly go to Nicaragua. Matthew Dyer, a young doctor from the UK, had mailed dozens of churches around the UK, asking for funds for a forthcoming visit he was making to Central America. We sent him the relatively small profit we'd made from a music concert the previous evening, and asked him to stay in touch. As a result, within twelve months I was flying with him and Nigel, another of our Northants pastors, to Costa Rica and Nicaragua in December 1989, at the very end of the Sandinista era.

Having been fascinated by the Soviet world since childhood, I found the culture of Soviet-backed Nicaragua to be utterly intriguing. What's more, I found the ministry of the Verbo Church totally inspiring. It was undoubtedly the most integral, holistic, community-connected church network I had ever seen. Despite getting sick on every trip, hating the food, being followed and investigated by the KGB, having to fly on dangerously old and badly-repaired planes over lethal thermals, and even once being held hostage by machete-wielding rum-fuelled Miskito Indians on the Mosquito Coast, I could never wait to make my next visit to Nicaragua.

On one such trip, whilst staying in Bluefields on the Atlantic Coast, Nigel and I were called one morning for breakfast. We came out of the damp wooden house onto the veranda outside, where the breeze – and by local parlance even the deadly Hurricane Mitch was called a breeze - provided just a little respite from the unrelenting humidity. We found that places had been set for fifteen people - family, farm workers, guests, passers-by – all were welcome at Ed and Ligia's table. At each meal there would be a choice of menu: rice and beans, or beans and rice. This morning it was rice and beans, but we were intrigued to notice that an egg had been placed on two of the fifteen plates that were laid out around the rough wooden table. Nigel and I commented together on how cute it was that this morning, alongside the rice and beans someone had managed to find an egg each for Ed and Ligia's two children. Nigel and I were the first to sit, and soon others joined us. But the children were not placed near the eggs. "The eggs are for *you*," they exclaimed to

Nigel and me, expressing surprise that we had not realised, and they insisted that we moved to sit in the two places where the eggs were set. Such poverty; such generosity. I'd never wept over an egg before, but unashamedly, I did that morning - and in fact have done many times since when telling that story.

We (Praise Community Church) funded the purchase of a vast expanse of farmland in Bluefields, complete with snakes and crocodiles, that overlooked the suffocating humidity of the Atlantic Ocean; land on which (to this day) many of the church's ministries and employment opportunities have their base, funded these days (amongst others) by Samaritan's Purse. In fact, it was whilst I was in Bluefields many years later (in 2003) that I first encountered Samaritan's Purse.

Over the next few years following my initial visit to Nicaragua, we sent prayer teams, work teams, English language teams and ministry teams to work alongside the Verbo Churches of Managua, Bluefields and Puerto Cabezas. Their founder leader, Bob Trolese, a Californian whose testimony is a book in itself, effectively became my big brother and mentor during this period of time. His wisdom and the holistic nature of his gospel have had a hugely positive influence on me.

Between 1989 and 1991, Praise Community Churches raised over £130,000 purely for these three overseas partner initiatives. At the same time the number of church staff members we committed to in the UK increased to 45. Quite extraordinarily, this was one in seven of the congregation at that time. It therefore required, on average, 15% of the average church member's salary just to pay the wages of the employed pastors, administrators, evangelists and musicians of the church. But apart from these commitments, we also ran and fully funded a full-time Bible College, a café and recording studio in North London, a sub-culture all-night church for disaffected youths in Kettering, and hosted expensive high-profile festivals for evangelism and experimental worship. We also had a number of buildings and building projects to maintain, all out of the tithes of the church.

Our musicians were wonderful. Music was another of the key ministries of the church, and they served as exceptional worship leaders, evangelists, and as sub-culture youth church leaders.

It was so dynamic. We thought it would last for ever, with the same focus and the same people. As far as I understood, I would be totally committed to everything we were doing for the rest of my life.

CHAPTER FOUR
DISASTER STRIKES

In December 1991 our family of four went abroad for two months on sabbatical. I recall Dan saying, "Go and see what God wants you to do for the second half of your life." With hindsight, I believe he had almost certainly decided by then what he was going to do with the second half of *his*. We spent a month around Christmas and the New Year with our friends and partners in Nicaragua. During this time my mother died, but due to the complexities of travel in that part of the world, I was unable to return for her funeral. My wonderfully patient sister and brother-in-law organised the funeral, and we returned home for a few days a couple of weeks later to help manage her estate, before going as planned to stay with our church in Belgium for another month. I turned 40 on 12 March 1992.

Less than two weeks later, at ten o'clock on the evening of 24 March 1992 (the eve of our son Ben's 14th birthday) I received the phone call that would change my life. It was Dan, phoning from London. His voice sounded shaky. "Alan, I think you'd better come down to see me in London. I've fallen in love with another woman." I was in total shock. After a restless night full of storm-tossed nightmares, from which I would wake from time to time and realise that the phone call *had* actually happened, I somehow briefly celebrated Ben's birthday with him over breakfast before dashing down to North London.

I was unable to persuade him to think again, and that darkest of days ended with Dan walking out from his wife, his sons, his church and his job. The last time I ever set eyes on him was when he struggled down the stairs from his apartment with one bulging suitcase.

That day we had ministry teams functioning in Sri Lanka, in Nicaragua, in Romania and in Switzerland. Dan's eldest son was a musician in the Switzerland team. When I had got my mind around the surreal facts, I called the leaders of each of these teams. I called all our local pastors around the country. I called Spring Harvest to explain that Dan would not, after all, be speaking at their conference the following week. I called key praying friends around the world. And during each call, another screw turned in the breath-taking band that was tightening like a ratchet around my chest.

So a network of spectacular, high-commitment churches in deep crisis fell into my lap overnight and by default. For me, despite my own feelings of shock and betrayal, two years of desperately intensive stabilising, decentralising and restructuring lay ahead.

At first, many of the 400 church members felt totally numb with shock. Then, after a couple of days, there was a rush to get personally cleaned up. People were repenting of anything they could possibly think of that they had ever vaguely done wrong. "If that could happen to Dan, what could happen to me?" In our shock we were desperate to be clean, to be open, to be safe. We were nervously in awe of the holiness of God.

A third stage quickly followed. It was a determination to rise up. "We can get through this. God is in His heaven. This will make us more determined than ever to love and serve Him." We had a period of mourning and repentance – I think it was about six weeks – after which we invited key leaders, friends and partners from all over the world as guests to a seven-day celebration we called a 'Week of Jubilee'.

Among these friends, all of whom supported me wonderfully in the two years that followed, were Martin Buehlmann from Switzerland, Gerald Coates and Mike Pusey from the UK, Bob Trolese from Nicaragua and Gordie Lagore from Canada. Such was their wisdom and support that I began to refer to them as my five apostolic friends. Mike and Bob fathered us with big generous arms of grace, wisdom and perspective. Gordie wept with those who wept, and God spoke through Martin with startling prophetic accuracy through the whole process. Even a month before Dan's departure, through a word of knowledge to the whole network of churches assembled one night in Harlow, Martin had publicly prophesied that somebody in the church was secretly considering leaving his wife, and that this was their last chance to confess and repent. Nobody responded, but I remember sitting near Dan, who had his head in his hands. All I thought at the time was how tired he looked that night.

One evening during that Week of Jubilee, Gerald came to speak to the whole network of churches. At one point in the meeting he talked to everyone about my role, about the gap that I had been forced to stand in, and for the need I would have of honour, prayer and support. He asked everyone to stand and express their commitment to me in an appropriate applause. All the people responded with a staggering wave of zeal and emotional release. On and on and on it went. Firstly I stood encouraged, then I stood relieved; I stood honoured; I stood embarrassed. Then I paced around the stage, not knowing how to stand anymore as the applause continued. After *eight* minutes I pleaded to everyone to stop. It was an overwhelming moment of time.

That week was a wonderful time. God washed over us with such grace and mercy. At last this nightmare had been dealt with. We were ready to emerge clean, humbled, restored, and ready to grow plenty more churches. Or so we thought.

However, despite this evident commitment to repentance, holiness and determination, in reality our new world started the day after the Week of Jubilee ended. Only then did the depth of people's sense of betrayal actually set in, and only then did people's determination to press on waver. I was forced to realise that this wildly enthusiastic, ridiculously generous, magnificently gifted band of pilgrims were anything but ready to move on. Shock, prayer, repentance, awe and resolve gradually gave way to caution, disappointment, resentment and blame.

I had never studied sociology, but God made it very clear to me that it would take two painful years before this group of churches could in any way be called stabilised, and perhaps five years before the bulk of its people would be truly healed and restored from the sense of betrayal they had suffered.

The money dried up, as did the enthusiasm, the ministry initiatives, and the lavish sense of worship. Day after day, week after week, month after month, I met with people who wanted answers, and who wanted to off-load blame, accusation and responsibilities onto others.

These were people who had sold their properties and made the proceeds available for the ministries of the church. Some of these families, now in their retirement, live today in small town-centre terraced houses, whereas they had once lived in wonderful, purpose-built properties in the country. Although there was never any question of Dan being involved in any financial irregularities whatsoever, some, understandably, felt deeply angry and wanted their money back. Despite often feeling quite numb emotionally, I recall sitting with several people and slowly helping them work through their frustrations, all the time making it my aim to put their focus and trust firmly back onto the faithfulness of the Son of God, rather than on the unfaithfulness of a man. This was not an easy task, either for me or for those I was seeking to support.

By contrast, most new believers shrugged their shoulders and more or less said, "Stupid man for doing what he did, but what is all the fuss about?" In truth, the longer people had been involved, the deeper their sense of betrayal. As they couldn't vent their anger at Dan, who had vanished, I became the next best target. As my wife said to me more than once after hearing such reactions, "They speak to you as though it was *you* that ran off with another woman!" A sense of utter deflation, depression and demoralisation set in. The generosity, the openness and the worship, the characteristics that had been such a wonderful mark of God's grace on our lives for so many years, imploded. It was like wading through treacle.

My mother had died just two months before Dan's fall from grace. Somehow my parents had saved money to give my sister and me around £14,000 each in their will. My inheritance was spent on stabilising the churches, by paying salaries and putting expensive structures in place to restore peace and order.

My five truly apostolic friends continued to stand alongside me during that time, supporting my leadership and vouching for my credibility. Gerald Coates and Mike Pusey, Martin Buehlmann, Gordie Lagore and Bob Trolese were lifesavers – but all lived many, many miles away. Increasingly I felt isolated, weary, defeated and heartbroken, but I carried on like a robot. The daily loneliness - something I had never experienced in the previous twenty years of community – the *loneliness*, especially as I walked into a building for a church meeting – often manifested as a tight band of pain across my chest that physically made me gasp; a groan in the depths of my heart.

The months went by. Some people moved on, to other towns, to other churches, all with my blessing and support. It wasn't that I wanted them to go, but I sensed that they just really needed a new start. One or two just drifted off through the pain of it all. I dismantled the structures that had become unhealthily dependent on Dan and his personality, and one by one sent all 45 full-time workers back to work elsewhere – a hugely painful process for many who felt so deeply called and committed to the functions they had been fulfilling. Many were musicians. Stuart Garrard went on to work with Delirious, and others with Graham Kendrick, Kevin Prosch, Iona and Alanis Morissette.

Through extensive consultation, I supported the appointment of new leadership teams in our churches in each town. In the process of time I encouraged some to look at, court with, and join with the Baptist Union, New Frontiers and Pioneer networks in UK, and others to merge with other local churches in their areas. I'd never dismantled a church network before.

In Dan's absence, and because people's anger tended to be focused on me, my wife eventually grew deeply weary with what we were doing and how we were living. After a few months - maybe a year - into the stabilising and decentralising process, something cracked inside her. She decided she'd had enough, and didn't want anything more to do with it all. She stopped attending church meetings. I was on my own, and it was agony. Mustering up the clear, sweet, faith-filled spirit necessary to lead a church with so many weary, cautious and hyper-sensitive people through stages of crisis *with* one's wife by one's side, would have been one thing. Trying to do it in the knowledge that I no longer had support from home was emotionally heartbreaking. Having had such a wonderful community around me for the whole of my adult life, being alone was a state that I'd had little experience of up till that time. It was an overwhelmingly lonely time for me.

I would regularly take time out and walk round Rutland Water. It was air to my lungs, an oasis of peace where I could seek the presence of God that I so needed. I paced this five mile circular track weekly, and weakly, for months. Painfully and over time, often spent praying and crying before the Lord, I recognised that God was asking me a simple question. "With whom is your primary human covenant? Is it with the church members, with your job, with your sense of calling?" However deep these things were, I had no doubt that the deepest relational call on my life was to my bride. And I knew that whatever the buzz, the success, and the sense of identity, vocation and fulfilment I had experienced in leading the church over the previous twenty years, and however determined I was to steer it through its present pain and lead it into a brave new era, God was asking me to lay it all down for the sake of my wife. So, with her agreement, I made what for me was an enormous decision.

Ensuring that new leaders were raised up and appointed in each location, I gave about nine months' notice and planned my careful departure from the leadership of the church. Two years to the day after Dan left (i.e. 25 March 1994), I became the final one of the 45 full-timers to leave the employment of Praise Community Church. During the few months it took to sell our house, I worked part-time at Kettering's Tourist Information Centre. I was by then well known in the town, and people would come in to the TIC, look at me and whisper to one another, "What's gone wrong with the church? Why is *he* working in here?" With Joel, now 18, deciding to stay on in Kettering, by early August my wife and I and youngest son Ben moved away to Ipswich, from where we looked after my frail parents-in-law, and where I found a job providing supported housing for homeless and vulnerable people.

Volunteering to walk away from the church I birthed and loved like a child, from my home, my town, my calling, my job, my friends, my familiarity, my identity, my history, my hopes and my plans for the future, was massive. I was voluntarily walking away from the fundamental building blocks of my life. I *grieved* for Kettering for several years.

So why did it go so wrong? Was it all about the relational and sexual immorality of one man, or were there reasons behind and roots beneath this final disastrous act that somehow made it inevitable? How could God allow so much to be built, only to let it collapse?

Well firstly, not everything collapsed. A quarter of a century on from Dan's fall from grace, hundreds of men and women who had been involved with Praise Community Church during those years continue to serve God around the world. From time to time I meet them and hear their stories. I rejoice in their faithfulness, their resilience, their determination to follow Christ. I praise God for the work they are doing, the churches they are leading, the NGOs they have founded, the businesses they are engaged in, the music they are playing, and the ministries they are fulfilling - ministries that God is pleased to continue to anoint for His glory. And when we have quiet moments to reflect on our shared past, we all agree that we have never seen local church quite like it, before or since, anywhere in the world.

Several of the churches we planted continue to walk faithfully with God, caring for one another and being salt, light and servants to their communities. A couple of others merged into other networks and ministries. A few, including the one in North London, were dealt too big a blow by Dan's departure, and one which they were not able to survive. We led them through as dignified a burial as possible.

There was no questioning the strengths of the Praise Community network, many of which I have outlined in this book: its shared life, its radical commitment to discipleship, its vibrant worship and use of gift, talent and music, its willingness to serve God and people, its bias towards the poor and vulnerable, its outstanding generosity, to name a few.

However, I believe the disastrous decisions made by the senior leader at that time exposed another fundamental weakness in the church. I think we had arrived at a place, collectively, where we actually believed all our own publicity. We were getting strong, with a confident and punchy outlook, and a robust opinion on anything vaguely connected to life and the Kingdom of God. We were becoming greatly in demand for speaking at conferences, especially about love, marriage and relationships in the church. We were loved, honoured and respected by many people all over the world.

Although it was one thing to *be* the most dynamic church in town, it was another thing to *know* it. I think we grew to love, not just God, but also the church, i.e. *our* church. Somewhere along the line, we fell in love not only with God but also with our own identity. It (the church) gave away everything it had, except for a pride in itself.

People who wanted to leave or move away from the church of their own choosing were treated at best with indifference or disappointment, whereas those whom the leadership sent out went with wholehearted support and celebration. We didn't connect brilliantly well with other local churches and, as I've already described, we had to come through a number of learning processes before we connected naturally or comfortably with our surrounding society. Maybe, just maybe, the church was a little too radical for its own good.

And so, after many years of reflection, I think power, control and pride were the fundamental issues. Take note, dear pastors and those who aspire to leadership. God will not share His glory with anyone else.

CHAPTER FIVE

IPSWICH

And so to Ipswich. We rented a couple of cottages for two or three months each, and then bought a house. It was a wonderful purchase – more house than we ever thought would have been possible, moving as we did from a run-down East Midlands terraced house to a detached house with 70 metres of secluded garden in Ipswich. The condition of the house and garden was not good, but we invested a lot of time and energy into making it more habitable, and at the time of writing, twenty-three years later, it is still my home, and I love living there as much as ever.

Joining with a local Christian community in Ipswich was difficult. Our aim was to look around for a church that would be similar in nature to what we had known in Northants, but soon we were forced to realise that this aim was unrealistic. The small Praise Community Church that we'd planted in Ipswich a few years earlier had decided during the decentralising process to merge with another church in Ipswich, and so this one became the obvious choice for us. We spent a year at this church, which on the face of it had a similar philosophy and approach to what we had known. However, although the people sincerely loved God and were very pleasant to us, we felt increasingly hemmed in and unfulfilled by the unbalanced and indigestible diet of meetings, meetings and more meetings that appeared to me to be the sum total of the church's vision.

Having spent the previous two decades perceiving local church as being (among other things) a lifestyle, a community and a commitment to neighbourhood services (be they providing a needle exchange facility for drug users in Kettering, or digging wells for clean water projects in Nicaragua), we found that to be presented with a 'meetings and buildings only' approach to local church was wearisome. Others in the church were becoming intrigued by our history, but we weren't really in a position to do anything more than tease people with what could have been. Being anxious not to upset the vision of the leadership team, and having explained to them how we felt, we slipped quietly out of membership.

It was to be almost five years before my wife and I would join another local church. Having spent weekends gardening, cycling, making one-off visits to churches, attending occasional conferences etc, we eventually started to attend Earl Soham Baptist Church, where the Greenbelt Christian Arts Festival was birthed many years ago. My wife was particularly cautious about committing herself to another church. In lighter moments we would joke together that she was so cautious about commitment that she wasn't even sure if she wanted to be a member of the *public*!

But Earl Soham Baptist Church was an incredibly laid-back village church situated about 14 miles north of Ipswich, and I having been born in the village, and my wife in the next village, we were accepted as long-lost friends.

I tried to personally maintain the Praise Community Church's financial commitments to Sri Lanka, Romania and Nicaragua (even though I no longer had the support of the church behind me), but after a few months I had to accept defeat. I recall the pain with which I had to tell each of these covenant friends that I could no longer raise the funds to underwrite their programmes – highly productive initiatives that had been such a central part of my life for a number of years.

But by 1996, two years after moving to Ipswich, I was desperate to see if God still had an international, cross-cultural call for my life. Whilst driving home from work one day, I heard a feature on BBC Radio Five where the speaker was appealing for people to join a fund-raising cycle trip from St Petersburg to Moscow. Not only would participants cycle the 600 kilometres in a week, but they would do so on tandems, with blind people on the back seats. A light went on inside of me, and in an instant I was determined to apply.

Having never possessed the ability to retain names, let alone telephone numbers, I nevertheless resolved to remember this one. Arriving home an hour later I contacted the organisation, and was accepted onto the trip. The fundraising (which included organising pub quiz nights and car boot sales) and the training (which involved signing up to gym membership for the only time in my life) took many months of energy and effort, but the trip itself, shared with over one hundred people, a number of whom were very hardened against and cynical towards Christ and Christian believers, was a wonderful experience. It was a new environment for me to exist in, and yet this experience gave me another great opportunity to demonstrate (to myself as much as to the other cyclists) that Christian believers could give themselves to such activities in a way that boldly and kindly proclaimed and demonstrated (in equal measure) the love of God. One evening the sighted rider of a gay couple fell sick, and he asked if I would support his blind partner through the intricacies of the evening visit to the local sauna. Walking stark naked and arm in arm with a blind man, while we poured hot water over one another and swacked each other with birch leaves, was not something I could recall ever having done before. Or since, come to that.

This sponsored cycle journey also gave me expression for a dream that I'd had since childhood – that of visiting what was now the *former* Soviet Union. I found that brief dip into the former Soviet culture to be utterly intriguing and exhilarating – emotions that would remain with me even many years later. But I could not have guessed at that time how wide the doors would open up for me into this part of the world almost a decade later. I'd still never heard of Samaritan's Purse.

After moving from Kettering to Ipswich, I worked for ten years in supported social housing provision for the marginalised. To begin with, I was slow to see how my experience as a pastor would help me do a job for a housing association, even one which (when stretching its imagination somewhat) regarded itself as Christian. My confidence had been shaken, and emotionally I was still coming to terms with the radical change of direction that my life had taken. But gradually I gained confidence that my previous skills and experiences really could transfer into the big bad world of public sector service.

Yet again, Felixstowe was to play a key part in my life. The job that I secured in that emotionally rootless August of 1994 required me to manage a new Supported Housing scheme for vulnerable people in that east coast town. A soulless old block of flats overlooking a cemetery, and a woefully inadequate budget for its renovation and for staff levels had already been approved. As the town had no other equivalent supported housing provision at the time, Social Services departments flung at me every sort of problem person for whom they had no answers. Their special needs were due to learning disabilities and mental ill health, and many of our service users were young people coming out of care. These young people, given a level of independence that they had not experienced before, just went *wild*, and we experienced many broken nights, drug raids, gun and knife attacks, and visits to police stations and hospitals. Sadly, some of those young people are no longer even alive anymore. Although they exploited the lack of staff numbers and the unsuitable layout of the building to fling their troubled selves at every excess imaginable, slowly, and through a lot of stress and anxiety, we managed to achieve a level of stability.

The organisation took note, and offered me promotion to a more regional role. I spent the next nine years overseeing other such supported housing schemes in Essex, Suffolk and East London. To this day I have some really good friends among those former colleagues, and for a time felt a measure of fulfilment through some of the responsibilities I was given. But overall, and at some point on most days during that time, I still had this gnawing thought in my mind, "Is this *really* what God has put me on earth to do?"

I recently found a poem I wrote during that time. Rather clumsily, I'd called it "Five years on, my own Psalm 13 (Some days only)."

> Is everything slipping away from me?
> It sometimes feels that way.
> For all the things I love to do
> And claim and justify are true
> I know there's something missing still.
>
> Should I have quit in '92,
> After Jubilee but before all the pain?
> Would that have rescued the mind and heart
> Of the one I love the most?
> Was I just playing a hero's game
> And shielding my heart with deceit?
>
> And really, will the sparkle ever return?
> The purpose, the public intimacy.
> And could it ever be the same

Or different but as good?
Certain words and goals I loved
Which seemed like jewels and eternal,
Now just die as dull thoughts in front of me
To be poked around with my toe in the dust
Of frustrated idleness.

But I love who I love and my loyalty's fierce
To Him, to the truth, to the just and the kind
And I ache and I'm restless and lonely and lost
And I want then I don't and then I don't know.

Two things are clear to me from reading this poem again. One is that I'm not a poet. The other is that I was still coming to terms with my recent past, and I hadn't got there yet.

One day I awoke to the slightly uncomfortable realisation that every one of the 60 staff members I was responsible for had greater qualifications than I had. My lack of any formal qualifications had never been an issue to me throughout my adult life, but now it felt good to seek from my employers some time out to study for a Post Graduate Diploma in Housing Studies. They were very supportive and so, accessing it on the basis of five years of housing management experience, I began a three year day-release course at Anglia Polytechnic University (now Anglia Ruskin) in Chelmsford. I found that to study at this level helped me hugely to think more strategically about society and its structures.

Not only was I the oldest and the least qualified student on the course, but as the course ended, I was also the only student who chose to go on to do a fourth year – which was an MSc in Housing Studies. During those first three years, I had won a couple of awards, which I reinvested into the funding of research trips to do case studies on housing provision in Nicaragua and in Kyrgyzstan, both of which were integral to the dissertation. The University awarded me what they told me was the highest grade they'd ever given in Housing Studies, and I'm pretty certain the certificate is still safely tucked away in some drawer or other at home. I found the whole experience very formative but, as I have never been that interested or comfortable in formality and occasion, the fact that the University completely forgot to invite me to the graduation ceremony was actually more of a relief than a disappointment.

But the most enjoyable aspect of my work with Shaftesbury Housing Association was the informal secondment I was imaginatively granted by the board of directors, which was to develop the Association's relationship with Habitat for Humanity International (HFHI). With Christian roots and values, Habitat was a self-build housing charity which had constructed more than 400,000 houses in over 100, mostly developing and transitional, countries around the world. Through an interest-free loan and with sweat-equity (an investment by future home owners of numerous hours of labour into the building of their own and their neighbours' simple, decent, affordable homes), those with small but sustainable incomes could achieve home ownership within about ten years.

Shaftesbury Housing Association had already donated land to Habitat for Humanity in Banbury for their initial UK project and, wanting to follow this up, they invited me to help develop the organisation's Global Village programme in the UK. Global Village was a short-term mission team programme whereby volunteer team members would go for a couple of weeks to work alongside those building their own homes. Shaftesbury very generously offered a large subsidy for employees to apply to go on these two-week trips to another country to assist with the Habitat house-building programme. This initiative quite naturally caught the imagination of many employees, and raised their staff satisfaction levels significantly. It also received a lot of positive press coverage both in trade journals and other media, and was used as a good practice model of how companies could invest creatively into their employees.

I was given the task of training and sending these short-term teams to different parts of the world. During this time I trained team leaders and team members in the UK, in Ireland and in Hungary, and personally led HFHI teams to Sri Lanka, Portugal, Nicaragua and Kyrgyzstan. Each was an amazing experience; not only were many houses built, but many long-term friendships were formed and many lives were positively changed. During this time some team members met with God for the first time, others who had become disillusioned returned to God, and one young man and young woman even fell in love and subsequently got married. Team members would often say how animated I was when leading these teams. "We've never seen you quite like this before," they would say.

One of my responsibilities with the team I led to Nicaragua was to return with a short film of the experience, which was to be produced professionally and used as a central feature in the Shaftesbury HA 30th anniversary celebration conference in Eastbourne. Exhausted and jetlagged from the trip, I worked long hours with a small team to produce this film within a few days (and nights), and just in time for the conference, where our leading guest speaker was Habitat for Humanity's American founder and president, Millard Fuller. That was probably my most fulfilling time with Shaftesbury Housing. Sadly, soon after that, new directors were appointed, men and women who didn't see the value of the Global Village programme, and who rapidly stifled both the funding and the Christ-like and incarnational influence it had.

Our sons had long since left home. Joel moved around fairly regularly, settling into teaching English as a foreign language in (among other places) Bishkek in Kyrgyzstan and Samara in Russia, and later, after meeting Ella, in Bratislava (Slovakia), Cambridge and Bournemouth. Having been unable to quite fulfil his teenage dream of becoming a mountain biking professional, Ben moved to South London to do a discipleship course with the Ichthus Christian Fellowship network. During this time he developed a love for dance, and met his wife-to-be Tope, who was also a dancer and choreographer. This remains their passion, calling and employment today.

Meanwhile, my wife worked as a nursery nurse, firstly at the local hospital, and then through medical centres into the community. Although she was nervous of being committed to a church, and couldn't really be said to be investing into a growing relationship with God, we nevertheless got on well, and had some common interests in cycling and gardening together.

However, in November 2003, it felt to me like something was rapidly dying inside her, particularly in respect of our relationship. A gnawing anxiety grew in my heart, and one day I found myself asking her what secrets she was holding from me. What decisions had she made recently? There followed a long and dreadful silence, and I could feel the most horrible cold sweat coming over me. It is not appropriate in this context for me to discuss the details, but enough to say that she had made a series of choices, decisions and relationships that were far removed from the ones we had been making as a young couple. Within six months, at the age of 50, and after 30 years of what was actually a very happy marriage, where we had stood side by side in mentoring community households, planting churches and leading marriage seminars, she left me to live with a man she met one evening at a nightclub.

Those six months were the most agonising in my life - far outweighing the pain of Dan's departure twelve years earlier. I spent many hours crawling over the living room floor, sobbing, wailing, and groaning my heart out, sometimes right through the night.

You must decide whether you think this was a strength or a weakness, but my cry to my Heavenly Father was never, "God, why have you let me down or deserted me?" Rather it was, "How will you get us through this?" His presence remained real despite the pain. I guess I really had settled something inside me when I was about twenty, and I was proving it to myself again now. What had I settled? That God truly *exists*, that He is altogether *good*, and that He *likes* me. When I tell people this, some have sounded disappointed, and have urged me to change the word 'like' to 'love'. Yes, I know God loves me. That's His job. But more than that, He also *likes* me, i.e. He's not embarrassed by me, and loves spending His time with me. If I go for a walk, or to work, or to football, He wants to come with me. If ten of us have to drive somewhere in three cars, Jesus comes and asks me if He can travel in *my* car. Such knowledge is too wonderful for me, and therefore even in this latest and most intense pain, there He was.

I have for decades loved what the Bible teaches about covenant – surely one of its central themes - and God's heart for the way all relationships are to be lived. When I am given the opportunity to speak in a church on a subject of my choice, I frequently choose to speak on covenant relationships. The whole concept of covenant is a deeply established foundation, theology and passion in my value system. It has been my way of life for decades. How extraordinary, then, that these two major life crises through which I had to travel, both revolved around the breaking of covenant by the two people closest to me. Or maybe this is not so extraordinary. If I didn't care about faithfulness so deeply, so passionately, I guess these crises would not have been so fundamental for me.

An excruciating life-crisis can take many forms. For some it involves coping with serious or debilitating sickness or injury. For others it could be an encounter with war, serious economic collapse, an irreparable injustice, or some other practical disaster. For others still (as was in my case) it is relational. It seems to me that for those who encounter it, crisis brings us to a fundamental crossroads, hence the expression 'the crux (the cross) of the matter'. I guess this is what Jesus was referring to in the parable of the sower, when the seed fell on the rocky ground, and "when trouble or persecution comes because of the word". I have seen crisis having the impact of pushing people into all sorts of wild and destructive decisions and, equally, I have seen it being the making of a person. 'Never trust a man without a limp' is an expression I have enjoyed for many years. After Jacob was left alone, and wrestled with God all night, he was left with two things. One was a dislocated hip, and the other was an extraordinary experience of the presence of God (Genesis 32). The damage that the dark night of the soul inflicts upon us can be gloriously outweighed by the depth of character and presence He puts in us – as long as we walk through that precarious journey faithfully trusting God. Despite the sometimes overwhelming sense of loneliness, betrayal, failure and rejection I felt at that time, I was deeply determined to walk with God and to have a future with Him.

CHAPTER SIX
SAMARITAN'S PURSE

Amazingly, at exactly the same time as I was journeying through this life-crisis, I also applied for employment with Samaritan's Purse, a Christian relief and development organisation best known (in the UK, at least) for its incredible children's Christmas gift-box programme, Operation Christmas Child (OCC). The night before my job interview was one of those nights of crawling around the floor, once more weeping my broken heart out. At about 6.00am I looked at my watch, dragged myself up off the floor, had a shower, and drove the 70 miles down the A12 to the interview at Buckhurst Hill.

If ever I needed a green light from God it was then, because those were days in which I didn't even want to step out of the front door, for fear of who would step in. And here I was seeking a job that would regularly take me all over the world. In what condition I presented myself for my interview I can only guess; but somehow in the grace, mercy and purposes of God, Samaritan's Purse offered me the post of International Partnerships Manager. Despite the turmoil that was going on inside me, I knew God was asking me to accept this job, which clearly involved an intense overseas travel schedule and complex liaison with national leaders in at least 30 countries. So, returning the keys of my brand-new Audi company car, and taking a 30% pay cut, I handed in my notice to Shaftesbury Housing Association and accepted employment with Samaritan's Purse. My wife actually left me a few weeks after the job started, and I divorced her six to nine months later.

So please, never think you need a neat and tidy life to do anything worthwhile, or anything for God. As the Bible says, "The *foolishness* of God is wiser than human wisdom, and the *weakness* of God is stronger than human strength. God chose the *lowly* things of the world and the *despised* things to nullify the things that are, so that no-one may boast before him" (1 Corinthians 1). Despite me feeling as lowly and as despised as I ever had done, God in His mercy chose that very time to open this amazing door for me.

I joined Samaritan's Purse in March 2004, as International Partnerships Manager. My job description was part pastoral, part strategic, designed to ensure that trust, relationship and sustainability were built into the partnerships the organisation enjoyed at that time in Eastern Europe, Asia, the Middle East and Africa. As a job, and as a lifestyle, I absolutely loved it, and through it felt more fulfilled, motivated and purposeful than at any other time in the last twenty years. I often referred to it as the best job in the world, and it proved to be a wonderful era of my life.

Operation Christmas Child (OCC) is a truly extraordinary programme. Many consider it to be the jewel in the Samaritan's Purse crown; the icing on the Samaritan's Purse cake. It is such a simple concept. Donors provide an empty shoebox decorated with Christmas wrapping paper, into which they place gifts such as toys, sweets, hats, scarves, educational supplies, and a toothbrush and toothpaste, and these are sent as a gift to marginalised children around the world. Since 2009 the programme has been complemented by a children's 12-lesson discipleship programme called 'The Greatest Journey', onto which more than 15 million children have enrolled. OCC had its roots in Wrexham, North Wales, where a family gazed with tearful compassion on the televised reports of babies rocking in their cots in the dire orphanages of Romania immediately after the 1989 revolution, and committed to putting a smile back on their faces. The project rapidly grew over the next few years, and these days more than eight million such boxes are collected annually and sent around the world (not only from the UK but also from nations such as Australia, Canada, Germany and USA) as an innocent, colourful gift of love from one family to another. During each of my fourteen years with Samaritan's Purse we sent on average over one million gift-boxes from the UK. One of my first jobs with Samaritan's Purse was to ensure that the boxes arrived in the right spirit, at the right time, and to the right child. To do this effectively, in each country where the boxes were sent, we developed national leadership teams (comprising of leaders and activists from different church denominations) which were responsible for the delivery of the gifts and the well-being of the programme in their country.

In my first few months with Samaritan's Purse I travelled a lot, meeting with colleagues and partners in countries as diverse as Armenia, Azerbaijan, Belarus, Bosnia and Herzegovina, Georgia, Mozambique, Romania, Russia, Serbia and the USA. Again and again I was amazed by the faithfulness, determination and grace that were so evident in the lives and ministries of those with whom I worked. With Operation Christmas Child underpinning most of these partner relationships, and with limited resources, a number of colleagues quickly became friends. I learned so much from these early visits: from God, from cultures, from people and from travelling. On one hand I repeatedly had to reflect on the complexity and diversity of different nations and cultures. On the other hand I was forced to acknowledge how massive an impact some of these Samaritan's Purse programmes had around the world, as a string of national leaders of NGOs, church networks and government ministers would seek me out and want to meet with me. Despite my personal frailty and bashed confidence, and despite never serving within the organisation in anything more lofty than a middle-management position, when I travelled overseas, and thus was the organisation's face or representative, I began to realise just how influential was this role that I had stumbled into.

As though it were yesterday I remember my first visit to Pata Rat, an informal Roma community near Cluj-Napoca in Romania.

> It is raining. Through the misted-up windows of the van I can make out derelict factories from a bygone Ceausescu era, their rusting skeletal features looking forlornly over the back road out of the city. Other than our vehicle, the only traffic is the occasional truck from the cement factory, and a pony and cart. This looks like the road to nowhere.

> Actually it's the road to Pata Rat (pronounced 'Patta Ruut') – 'the fields of the village of Pata'. No arable land here though. No meadows or orchards either. Nothing green to be seen. The only crop in the fields of the village of Pata is rotting garbage. This stretch of land, between railway track and road, is the city's rubbish tip.

Here live and work one hundred Roma families, in the most appalling conditions I have seen in Romania. It's as dire as the tips in the large tropical cities of the developing world, but tropical this climate is not. Winter temperatures here drop to as low as minus twenty degrees. Mothers of young children – their faces aged and spirits broken by rejection, abuse and utter hopelessness – tell me how thick (three inches) last winter's ice was inside their cardboard and scrap homes. Their children cough with a hacking, cackling regularity. Many have tuberculosis or other lifestyle and respiratory sicknesses. Last winter a number of the children died. "He has a cold," one mother tells me.

Towing a trailer of the city's garbage, a tractor arrives on site, followed by excitable children and hungry dogs, running to see what can be salvaged from today's offering. Today the driver is restrained by city and police officials who swoop from nowhere to check out the black market deal that the driver is negotiating with the community. Once sorted, the salvage that is not edible – and I can see a tiny child in its mother's arms sucking on the remains of what looks like a glue stick – will make its way back to the city in their *chariot* (pony and cart). This is the residents' desperate attempt to make a few *lei* on the scrap plastic and wood.

When poverty is so deep, so all-consuming, generationally so long-term, it is often referred to as grinding. Grinding poverty. And it starts to drizzle again.

A violent argument breaks out between the wife of one family and the man of another. He turns out to be the community leader. She claims to be pregnant and sick, and unfit to sort through the garbage. "Then don't expect any of the takings," he shouts back. The body language is tight and livid – the rage of sheer and hopeless frustration.

I go to speak with an old lady who lives in a caravan donated by our partners, Ecce Homo. Albeit tiny (3m x 2m) and old, it stands out as smart in comparison with the shacks that surround it. But the old lady begs not to have to spend another winter in the caravan. "It was so bitterly cold," she tells me, "I would rather die than live in here again next winter." She looks to be in her seventies.

I ask her where she had previously lived. "I exchanged my home for another in the city," she replies, "which turned out to be owned by the city, who then evicted me. My income is nil. I have a daughter at school (first shock). I'm not old enough for state pension (second shock!), and because I'm a gypsy no one will employ me. They say I'll steal from them."

"How do you live then?" I ask.

"Occasionally my sister will give me something." She pleads for a new home.

Into this community last autumn ten very simple insulated steel dwellings were erected, in a partnership between Ecce Home and Samaritan's Purse. They wintered well. We plan to build another 40 this year. These will only scratch the surface of the multiple needs of this rejected and abandoned community, needs that include basic education, income generation, health and even identity.

"But what do we do?" asks Liviu Balas, the director of Ecce Homo. "Provide a lot for a few, or a little for all? This little (house) is a massive amount for these families. It's given them their dignity back, and opens up the possibility for employment."

Previously the men stank so badly of the burning tyres they used for keeping warm, that no one would ever want to employ them. A small handful of the men now work as janitors, and Ecce Homo has provided advocacy and support for a few others to be registered with the government. For the first time in their lives, this gives them a formal identity and enables them to access benefit entitlements, education and primary medical services.

I visit the tiny new home of one family – mother, father, two children, and one three-week-old grandchild. There's no power (although the city has now promised to provide electricity), there's no bathroom, no toilet, no sewerage. Incongruously, stinking soggy garbage is dumped within two metres of their white UPVC front door. The self-installed stove has caused health problems so it has been repositioned outside, where it doesn't cook properly. But the house is noticeably warm, and completely dry and draught-free.

"If you could change just one small thing about the house and its design," I ask the mother, "what would it be?"

"Nothing," she replies, with a warm sparkle in her eyes. "It's wonderful."

Jesus said the poor we would always have with us. He didn't say that they would always be content with the simple things, or always be grateful. But certainly some of them are.

Broadly speaking my role was to monitor the quality, effectiveness and value for money of the programmes Samaritan's Purse were funding. I would also train, equip and troubleshoot, seek out new partnerships, and accompany UK donors and TV or film crews for more promotional purposes. So the purpose of each overseas trip varied considerably, as did the environment, culture and climate of each destination. Whilst one week I might spend time in urban Eastern Europe with the Roma community, the very next week I could be getting to know a village chief next to crocodile-infested rivers in rural Mozambique.

Salomao Chicanequisso Cuinica is the Community Leader in the village of Nhampugnaune, in Guija District, Gaza Province, South-Western Mozambique. Nhampugnaune's 2,300 people are spread across four barrios or districts. Each barrio has a secretary who reports to Salomao.

I met Salomao at the World Food Programme monthly food distribution in the village, managed by Samaritan's Purse. He was overseeing the event, ensuring equity amongst the twenty-five participant families. This is how it works: at least one family member has to work for a minimum of three hours a day on a Samaritan's Purse food-for-work programme, such as building a dyke to access fields across a flood plain, or cultivating a seed multiplication initiative. In exchange, the family receives a monthly food package consisting of maize (75kg), yellow split peas or beans (7.5kg), and 3.7 litres of Soya bean oil.

Some families live on this alone – I'd just witnessed both their payday and their monthly shopping trip, all rolled into one. Other families have a little meat, I was told. Indeed, I saw the evidence of this myself. As I walked around the village, I saw one large fish cut open and left to dry on the straw roof of a mud house, and about fifteen to twenty charcoaled rats waiting for preparation outside another. Even the empty Soya bean oil cans themselves come in useful. Six or eight of them had been beaten flat and made into the door of one family's little circular mud-and-thatch hut.

There was no electricity in the village, but the government had promised to supply it. *"When* did they promise?" I asked. "Oh, years ago," came the reply. Malnutrition levels in Gaza are showing worrying levels of 11%. The official figure for HIV/AIDS in the country is 1.4m, with 13% of 15 to 49-year-olds living with the virus. But come to Gaza Province and the official figure becomes 19%, the highest infection levels in the country. Local district estimates put it at more like 50%.

The previous owner of Salomao's jeans was clearly an entirely different shape from him. His ancient vest was full of holes. I guess his attire was a reflection of his financial status. Salomao Chicanequisso Cuinica was not a rich man. He also looked like a man on whose kindly shoulders rested many a care. An observant man, I thought, though a man of few words. But with the food distribution over, he was happy to tell this strange white visitor to his village something of his life and aspirations.

Appointed as Community Leader in 1976, just twelve months after independence, Salomao witnessed Mozambique slide into civil war. The village of Nhampugnaune was on the front line. The fighting was bitter, and atrocities were committed on a massive and horrific scale. One of Salomao's early tasks was to lead his community to safety, across the Limpopo River to the nearby town of Chokwe. It was six years before they returned. Upon venturing back, Salomao re-established the village in a position he considered was far enough away from the river to protect it from flooding, but close enough to access the water for crop irrigation. "It's a good place to be," he told me.

Droughts followed. Then floods. Either way the crops failed. Salomao couldn't remember the years. But he remembered 2000. While the West mopped its collective brow with relief on discovering that its computers had survived the Y2K scare, the inhabitants of Guija District had other things on their minds. On 27 February, 2000, the Limpopo burst its banks. In the few hours that followed, 700 people died. A total of two million were affected. Around here, it is spoken of as "the time of the floods", perhaps more accurately written as "the Time of the Floods". Capital T, capital F.

The flood water stopped just short of the village Salomao had repositioned. There was no proud smile upon his face when he told me this, but I think maybe his shoulders went back just a little. His people were spared their lives. But of course, their harvest was not so fortunate. 2000 was yet another year of nil return.

So Samaritan's Purse opened a field office in Guija, providing simple and appropriate relief initiatives such as water filters, seed multiplication, food for work programmes and HIV/AIDS awareness training. The transition from relief to development is well under way. The hand-out is giving way to the hand-up.

I asked Salomao what were his major concerns for the future of Nhampugnaune. His replies were clear, simple and realistic. He wants a well for the school, in order to save the children from having to walk such a long way for water. And he looks forward to the day when each family in the village has a water filter.

I realised with a degree of embarrassment how Western my questions were. "When were the worst drought years?" He didn't remember the year. "How many families in the village have a water filter now?" He didn't know. "Quite a few now," he thought. I sensed him looking at me inquisitively. "Why is this white man so obsessed with mere numbers?" But I continued. "How often were people sick before they used the water filter compared with now?" Again, he didn't know. All he knew was that they used to be sicker than they are now. Fair enough. So much for my quantifiable research!

Just before I left in the back of the Samaritan's Purse 4WD, I gave Salomao a tiny token gift from the UK. And I realised he had come out of his shell a little. He put his arm round a young lad's shoulder, and his weary burdened face gave way to a big smile. Then he raised his arms above his head and applauded our departing vehicle, rather like a substituted footballer acknowledges the crowd. Against the odds, over maize and rats, through conversation and respect, we'd somehow connected. But the next monthly shopping trip is still a full moon away.

CHAPTER SEVEN
MANIC TRAVELS

From the start of my employment with Samaritan's Purse, my travel schedule was manic. For the very first time in my life I was living on my own. For the next five years, I would, on average, step onto a plane for another flight every six days. This intense travel schedule didn't *begin* to calm down for at least three years. My sons and their wives, and particularly my sister (who would contact me with precious care and attention several times a week, irrespective of where in the world I was, and tell me regularly that the only thing she worried about was that I'd fall asleep when driving home from Heathrow) were hugely supportive during this time, but the reality remained that I would return week after week to an empty house, which was little more than a functional base; bed, laundry, microwave, and springboard for the next trip.

On one occasion it took me 69 hours to make the journey to Gambia and (on the same trip) 51 hours to return home to the UK. I was stuck in Dakar (Senegal) for two days while a regional airline told me their flight to Gambia, on which I was booked, was cancelled due to a bird strike. A collapsed bridge prevented me from doing this leg of the journey overland. Consequently I missed (and hastily reorganised) the essential OCC meetings which were the purpose of my visit. Eventually the airline confessed that there was no bird strike – they'd just been offered a better deal by chartering the plane to a businessman. After my hastily rearranged meetings in

Banjul, I returned to the airport, only to find all the lights off. A security guard emerged from the gloom, confirming that there were no more planes leaving Gambia that night, and sent me away. I spent most of that night searching out the airline director, and upon finding him wining and dining, I asked him most assertively what he was going to do about getting me home. Legally, he was only obliged to get me as far as Senegal, but I must have sounded threatening enough, because he acted promptly and I was on my way. But in fact it wasn't just Senegal, or even just home that I needed to get to. Almost immediately after arriving home to the UK I was due to leave again for Canada, to lead Gordie and Kathleen's Vancouver Vineyard church weekend in the spectacular North Shore Mountain wilderness of Mount Seymour Provincial Park, British Columbia.

I recall eventually making it home from Gambia, and robotically putting the key in the door, dragging my luggage through to the kitchen, and stuffing my clothes straight into the washing machine, even before taking my coat off or making a cup of tea. Within twelve hours I was off again, headed for Canada. But this was not an isolated occasion. I had to plan and make use of every minute, just to keep to the schedule. Somehow, in the grace of God, I continued to live like this without having a breakdown.

Many trips were with colleagues and partners, but many more were undertaken alone. For someone who so fundamentally loves community, I found that I actually enjoy my own company as well, and was completely content when having to travel alone.

In my fourteen years with Samaritan's Purse I went on 154 trips, involving 572 individual flights, and visited 77 different countries and territories. Once I visited four countries in one morning. The countries I returned to most frequently were Kyrgyzstan (31 times), Belarus (17 times), Azerbaijan (15 times), Ukraine (15 times) and Rwanda (10 times).

My travels took me on some amazing road and rail trips, in all climates and conditions. Near to one of Saddam Hussein's Palaces in Northern Iraq, my vehicle got stuck in a one metre deep snow drift, with live mines on one side of the road and a sheer drop on the other. The following day I drove in baking heat to within 15km of the ISIS front line at the height of the conflict. I have driven through the debris of a 40m high avalanche in Kyrgyzstan, and survived landslides in the mountains of Azerbaijan and earthquake aftershocks in Nepal.

Sometimes I would write an account of my actual travel experience whilst still on the road – stories for example of the time I spent three days with no food in a totally empty hotel in Bosnia, or of the three days it took to get home from the Kyrgyz-Chinese border with a raging temperature and something I could only describe as yak flu. These journals, as in the case of the one below, were as much about the journey and the experience as they were about the purpose for my going.

Tuesday 18 November 2008

After an uneventful journey from Heathrow to Sheremetyevo (Moscow), my colleague Alex and I boarded our connecting flight to Bishkek from the dour Terminal F at 21.30. Forty-five minutes later we were told to get off the plane and wait in the lounge again. There was fog in Bishkek. We were put in two groups: those with visas and those without. Follow me. Wait here. Follow me. We meekly followed Aeroflot's bright young administrator as she circled the transit lounge a couple of times, finally bringing us back to the spot on the first floor from whence we had begun.

As their husbands hung back, struggling to look more dignified than bewildered, a gaggle of Kyrgyz women decided it was time we saw some action. Poor weather conditions a thousand miles away there might have been, but having flown already from Eastern Russia, these women had decided it was time that young Natasha should sort things out.

But this wasn't the first or the second time that young Natasha had been round this particular block. "Oh, don't get so excited. You've been travelling six hours already? Whatever! I've been here in this flipping airport for years. You remember the 1980 Moscow Olympics? Well nothing's changed since then. Not a *thing*!"

Wanting to be an encouragement to her, I politely pointed out that this was not strictly true, as the security checking system had been turned at right angles even since my previous visit in the summer, and the ceilings were being renovated as we speak; new plastic, albeit more flimsy, replacing the old. But from the mock scornful look she gave me, these were obviously not comforts that she as an Aeroflot staff member felt particularly benefited by. "Hmm," she said, in perfect English. And turning to address the complainants again, she concluded. "So don't moan at me. It's not foggy here, is it?"

Thank you for flying Aeroflot. Have a nice day (or night, or whatever it is now).

Wednesday 19 November 2008

We waited for another hour. At twenty past midnight we were told to go downstairs. As we went down the stairs, an equal number of travellers, also from our flight, who earlier had been shepherded in another direction, were being instructed to go from downstairs to upstairs. Well I suppose that's fair. I'm not sure we ever saw them again, but maybe I'm confused.

Our downstairs party waited patiently, then impatiently, and then one of the women started shouting obscenities at any unfortunate passer-by who looked vaguely like an airport employee. Then she just shouted obscenities, even when nobody passed by.

At ten past one we were taken in a bus to a nearby hotel. This noble establishment was in Russia proper, just outside the airport, but having no visa, we were kept under strict security at all times. After checking in (our passports were taken from us) we were taken ten at a time under the nervous supervision of guards who discussed our progress with unseen colleagues by walkie-talkie, to rooms off a particular corridor on the fifth floor. The door from the corridor was locked but the guard remained by it. Later we were given water and the promise of a meal. "And be ready to leave at 5.00am."

I dozed and waited, but wasn't convinced that the meal would come. Hungry but even more tired, I eventually dozed off, but in an instant was woken by a loud knock on the door. Two girls, accompanied by a guard, delivered a vaguely warm meal of spinach covered in salad cream, a *cutlet*, rice and bread, in a plastic container, and a plastic cup with a tea bag in it. "Hot water will come later." It didn't, so I settled down to sleep. It was 2.40am.

I set the alarm for 4.30am and showered. I waited by the guard, who waited by the locked door, and who struggled to tell me we would now leave at six o'clock. I went back and dozed again on the bed, then at 5.37am a shouted command in Russian came from along the corridor. "Come quickly, the bus is ready *now!*" Passengers of the delayed Moscow to

Bishkek flight SU 179 stumbled sleepily from their rooms. Two women giggled through their vodka-fuelled haze.

We waited in the corridor. We waited in the lift. We waited in the lounge. Every room we entered was locked behind us. Ways of absconding were limited. We considered forming an escape committee, but all hopes of liberty appeared to be lost, so instead we meekly queued to get our passports back. We waited again in the lounge. We waited on the bus. We boarded the plane. We took off at 8.00am.

We were asked to stand (or sit) and wait in a total 23 places in Moscow. Pieces of paper - tickets, passes, forms etc - numbered eight.

I slept heavily for an hour on the five-hour flight to Bishkek. With wheels lowered ready for landing, and the ground looking close, the pilot (we were later told) had clearance to land. However, at the last minute we hit thick fog and with a sudden and noisy thrust the plane soared back up in the air. Sitting facing us was one of the cabin crew. Her eyes widened and she grabbed the emergency instruction card. Had she been off sick on the day of the emergency landing training? Ten minutes later we were told that we would be landing in Tashkent (Uzbekistan) due to the density of the fog in Bishkek. This we did at 4.30pm Bishkek time (3.30pm Uzbek time). It would soon be dark again, and we realised we would be there for some time.

"May we have some water please?" asked Alex a member of the cabin crew, in a slightly pathetic, Oliver Twist sort of way. "We've run out of water," was the reply. Boredom set in. I sought to relieve the monotony by taking photos of Uzbek runway tarmac out of the open rear door of the plane, and discussed the merits of Abramovich and Chelski with the drunk who had loudly developed that state of inebriation right outside my prison door in Moscow the previous night.

We were still patiently sitting in the plane as darkness fell over Tashkent. We had been told that the pilot was discussing fog with the Aeroflot representative in the terminal. At least that was what we understood from the only English-speaking flight attendant. "It's very very fog in Bishkek."

The same attendant spoke again at 6.20pm. "Ladies and gentlemen, please take your hand luggage and run." I think he meant leave for the terminal, but for a moment I wondered if the Uzbeks had objected to our presence in a slightly more hostile way than the hospitable Russians the night before. Anyhow, running was out of the question, as they only let us through each door ten at a time.

As we climbed onto the transit bus, I realised we had already been under hotel arrest, airport arrest, and plane arrest. What would Tashkent have in store for those of us who had no visa?

We were taken to the transit lounge, which was tall and colonial, a cross between Islamic and Soviet 1950s architecture. A grand staircase rose with grace and elegance up the centre of the building, and pillars with elaborate décor held the two floors in place. Dusty, old, red, but once-plush carpets lined each walkway. At the top of the stairs, in the one room on the left were a few handmade wooden check-in desks with a basic, aging, grubby computer on each. The room to the right was a café, and from the look on their faces when they saw our line of weary, bedraggled, dehydrated, hungry travellers, the two young men behind the bar realised it could be worth them staying open over-night tonight. This was not the look we had wanted to see on their faces.

Passengers flocked around the old desk of the one Aeroflot representative who dared to show her face. The occasional announcements that were made were not translated into English. From time to time in the protracted negotiations we would press forward and ask the girl for an interpretation.

After a couple of hours most of the passengers (those with Russian or Kyrgyz passports and those with Uzbek visas) left on another bus to a hotel for the night. About 40 of us were left in the airport. Alex and I were the only Brits, and we were joined by Tajiks, an American, Germans, Finns and a Pakistani. Later we were to be joined again by a few others. Two were Kyrgyz missionaries who despite their Central Asian passports were sent back to the terminal without explanation. Another girl was sobbing her heart out. Apart from being rejected from the hotel, she had also received a phone call to say that her father had just died in Bishkek. We would all have to stay in the transit lounge until the fog lifted from Bishkek.

It wasn't obvious at first, but slowly we realised there was a kitchen behind the bar of the café, and someone made what is the classic rice-based

Uzbek meal of *plov* for us all. It was delicious. Just as we sat back in a chair replete, a very purposeful and jolly Aeroflot rep breezed in and victoriously announced that they would provide us with a meal after all.

Thursday 20 November 2008

By midnight there was still no sign of the meal we no longer needed, so after talking with the missionary ladies (who were returning from a church-planting trip to Tbilisi) we attempted some sleep. Fifteen minutes later I concluded that sleep didn't work very well when trying to twist myself round severely designed metal seat frames, so I read my book - 'Playing the Moldovans at Tennis' - instead. But with my ears ringing through sheer lack of sleep, I couldn't concentrate for long, so when our guards weren't looking I crept behind the check-in desk, found a rickety old wooden chair, took off my jumper and used it as a pillow on the desk. Perfect. 2.00am and the night is yet young.

Six minutes later a loud announcement was made in Russian, involving the word Bishkek. I looked up and the room was empty. Great, I thought. The fog had cleared and we would be off soon. I hurried to find my travelling vagrants, and found all 40 of them (but no Alex) eating breakfast in the café. Thinking Aeroflot were even providing breakfast before taking us back to the plane, I searched in dark corners of the transit lounge till I found the sleeping Alex, and woke him with the good news.

Slowly we realised that we weren't about to leave, and this was not breakfast. This was last night's meal, the one we didn't need. Duped again, we nevertheless squeezed together on tables of ten, and ate. The atmosphere was one of resigned and sleepy camaraderie. We even took a few group photos. But at 2.20am I tore myself away from the party and went back to my check-in bed, trying not to catch the eye of an Uzbekistan Airline employee who was now sitting nearby.

"Nyet." He was big, grumpy, but above all, overwhelmingly ugly. "Are we about to leave then?" I asked. "No, not till nine o'clock" "Well it's only 2.20am now," I reminded him. "Why can't I sleep here?" "Because we're about to start checking people in for other flights."

Fair enough, really. I guess it could have been a little tricky checking people into Uzbekistan Airlines early flight from Tashkent to St Petersburg with a long Englishman curled up, greasy and snoring on the check-in desk, so I found a piece of carpet at the top of the grand staircase and tried to sleep once more. It was 2.47am.

Three flights arrived in quick succession. From Kuala Lumpur, Tel Aviv and somewhere in Pakistan. The transit lounge became packed, and there was no longer room on the carpet (let alone the check-in desk) for an aging dozing vagrant. By this time Alex had given up his attempts to sleep as well, so for the next three hours, with heads nodding and twitching, we watched all the goals in the Spanish and English leagues on the TV, sat, read, and nodded some more. The smoke was thick, and apparently, so still was the fog in Bishkek.

We were back on the plane by 10.00am. They let us, the un-chosen few, onto the plane first, and soon we were joined by the remaining passengers, who looked and smelled like they had slept, cleaned their teeth, eaten, showered, changed their clothes, and probably even had a massage, a sauna and a swim. The cabin crew sheepishly smiled at us to test our mood, and then treated us like old friends just released from a long term of imprisonment.

We left Tashkent at 11.30am and arrived at Bishkek an hour later. The journey had taken 48 hours.

CHAPTER EIGHT
AN AMAZING WEEKEND IN GEORGIA

could see that there was much work still to be done to ensure that the programmes Samaritan's Purse was investing in would remain sustainable and Christ-centred. Having followed in the steps of a very dynamic and pioneering predecessor, I found that many doors were already wide open to me. Some of these opportunities, however, would clearly never achieve what my very mission-focused job description required of me, and I knew my main contribution would once more be towards a stabilising and strategic impact. I prayed (and I continue to pray) that God would help me to be a *culture-former*, and I used my pastoral history and my love and respect for the local church to seek to strengthen Samaritan's Purse's church-based partnerships, and to help the organisation move on as graciously as possible from those which could best be described as purely humanitarian. This was not easy, as from some of these relationships came such wonderful grace and hospitality, as for example the kindness that was lavished upon me during a weekend I spent in Georgia.

Friday 7 May 2004

Along with a dusty line of motorbikes, buses, chickens and watermelon, we approached the Azerbaijan-Georgia border just at the changing of the customs guard. Officers completing their duty kissed those who had come to replace them. I'd never seen that before, either at Heathrow or at Gatwick. Over the next hour we successfully negotiated six stages of border crossing and six closed gates to complete the entry process.

I'd only been with Samaritan's Purse a couple of months, but this was my fifth trip overseas, and my ninth country. Although the original purpose of my visit to Georgia was purely in order to transit between Azerbaijan and Armenia, I had been warned that their hospitality was second to none. But I hadn't been warned enough.

I should have guessed right from the start. Nana Loladze, the Head of the Georgian Red Cross Society and her chauffeur Leri had driven five hours down to Mingachevir in Azerbaijan just to pick me up. And now, arriving at the border, having already having been treated to a meal near Ganja, she insisted on paying for my $80 visa.

Neither Nana nor Leri spoke English, and I didn't speak Russian or Georgian. The journey we made from Mingachevir to Tbilisi was the first of many silent journeys I have made across vast swathes of the former Soviet Union. Nowadays, at least I can stumble through a mildly pathetic repertoire of left, right, toilet, quickly, please, chicken, potatoes, receipt and thank you in broken Russian.

So it obviously wasn't the charm of my conversation. Maybe it was my silent charisma, or my aftershave, or more likely just my sense of lost bewilderment - I was also very thin in those days, which despite my great age, often seemed to activate the caring mother-gene in many women I met. When we arrived on that pleasant Friday evening at the Red Cross headquarters in Tbilisi, however, a translator was summoned to break the five-hour silence. "We *had* arranged for you to stay at a hotel," he informed me, "but Nana says she likes you, and so this weekend you will stay in her family home."

Nana's home turned out to be simple, on the third floor of a typical nine-storey block on the northern edge of town. *Perestroika* had brought warmth and comfort to the apartment, and I learned that this was purely the family's temporary accommodation whilst their more palatial home was being completed.

I was given the master bedroom, and sat quietly on the bed. For the previous week I'd been working on a building site in Azerbaijan, constructing a play-park for the children of a settlement of Internally Displaced People (IDPs) in Mingachevir, and my colleagues had been a raucous team of footballers from Liverpool. Now let's be honest; I hadn't really understood much of their conversation either, but at least I had been able to console myself that despite the often impenetrable wall of Scouse, I had actually recognised a few sounds that had issued from their mouths. At least they had been speaking English of a sort. We'll say nothing of the sounds they had emitted at night. Suffice it to say I had shared a bedroom with 17 of them.

But now they and their unique and infectious team camaraderie were many miles away, and I missed them. This was different. I unpacked my mostly dirty clothes, and some of my bewilderment. This was very kind of Nana, but at least in a hotel I could have walked, slept, smiled at waitresses and pointed at things to eat in restaurants, and as such the weekend would have passed by fine. But staying here, I would have to socialise, understand the etiquette, eat whatever I was given, and sit in self-conscious silence.

Nana's husband Nicolai was the head of one of the leading Georgian television companies. He appeared at home soon after I arrived, and while I was still unpacking my emotions. We gave each other a strong handshake, nodded encouragingly if a bit repetitively to one another, and I *think* he said welcome. But then, after this most gregarious of starts, the conversation took a bit of a dip. Nodding twice more, I retreated into *his* bedroom.

But then things began to look up. Two more family members came home. No one had told me that Nana had two beautiful teenage daughters. Natia (18) and Tatia (13) were delightful, and practised their English on me with enthusiasm. Natia had spent a year learning English at a private school in the UK; she was sleek, sophisticated and classy. "Next time, when you bring your family, we will go to the coast," she told me. "Your son must come and live here." Tatia just beamed, and bouncing with Tiggeresque enthusiasm, she took me under her wing. I felt like I was the new puppy that her mother had just brought home. I hoped I wouldn't misbehave in the corner.

That evening we ate a simple meal in the kitchen before squeezing into Niko's car for a trip to view a local monastery near Tbilisi. It was dark, and quite late, but the view of the city lights was great. This looked to be a very exciting place.

Saturday 8 May 2004

It wasn't intentional. It just happened to be the eighth of May, World Red Cross Day, when I was passing through Tbilisi. To celebrate the occasion, Georgia Red Cross Society had planned several prestigious events, including an afternoon conference on HIV and AIDS at which the country's First Lady would speak, and a classy evening concert involving top musicians and performers. Despite being presented as a special overseas guest, I felt more like a bemused misfit who had been lavishly swept up whilst inadvertently passing by. If only I'd had a little less mud clinging to my combat trousers and tee shirt!

But at least my clothes suited the first project of the day, which was to clean up the play-park equipment that Samaritan's Purse had funded and built two years previously in Digomi, a District of Tbilisi where 40% of the population are Abkhazian IDPs.

Under the watchful eye of the national TV cameras, up to 50 Red Cross volunteers and staff members got stuck into cleaning and painting the colourful and creative equipment, the benches and the railings that protected the park from the busy road nearby. Clearly the equipment had been appreciated. It was well used, but was standing up well to the rigor of children's play. And refreshingly, hardly a word of graffiti was to be seen.

I spent a couple of hours there, watching, cleaning, occasionally talking with English speakers, and doing an interview for this evening's national TV news. I was also chatted up by a drunken *babushka* who, thrusting one of her rings onto my finger, declared (through Natia's suave interpreting services) that "All of Georgia loves you." "All of Georgia has hardly had time to *meet* me," I thought, risking offense by graciously returning the ring. "I've only been here about sixteen hours."

With the hot sun beating through the dappled shade of the trees, local residents joined the volunteers with brooms and paintbrushes. I chatted to some of the families who regularly used the park. One shy grandmother – Dodo was her name – ignored the bustle around her and gently and contentedly pushed Luka, her four-year-old grandchild, on a swing. "It's the only place like this in the district. I visit here with my grandson every three days," she told me. "If the city had another *six* places like this that would be very good."

A young couple weaved their way through the trees, their two youngsters squeezed in one small and aging buggy. They all looked mystified as to what the fuss and cameras were about. Dima and Nana Tskhvaradze prized their daughter Ala (almost three) and their son George (18 months) out of the buggy, and found some room for them on a climbing frame and a slide. "We're very content with this place," said Dima.

"It's not just a nice place, but a *necessity*," Nana added, stressing the final word. "We visit very often. There's no other place like this where we can go as a family." I smiled. We all need our little oases – the simple things we like to do together on a sunny Saturday morning. Things we still talk about with great affection decades later. Normality can be a wonderful thing.

The potholed road through the transitional world is littered with the projects of good intentions, and which relief and development agency has not made a few embarrassing errors of judgement in assessing the on-going perceived needs of a community? It was therefore heartening to see this Samaritan's Purse project very much alive and well two years on, and valuable beyond measure to discover that Dodo and Luka and the Tskhvaradze family found their oasis of happiness in a play park. And all credit to the Georgia Red Cross Society, on a day when they had to entertain many dignitaries in government and the arts, all under the critical eye of the national TV news, that their first priority was the slightly less glamorous task of maintaining a play park.

After a quick lunch we dashed off to a city-centre hall, where Red Cross was hosting a conference, cum concert, cum seminar on HIV and AIDS. Combats and tee-shirt might have worked fine whilst renovating the play-park, but I had to admit to feeling more than a little under-dressed for the remainder of the day. The main speaker at the HIV gig was Sandra Roelofs, the Dutch-born First Lady of Georgia. I tried with a degree of success to play down my 'special overseas guest' role.

"Later we have a really special treat for you," declared Nana as we waved goodbye to the President's wife. "We have tickets for a top Georgian singer's 60th birthday concert. But first, Niko wants to show you where he works".

So with him and a couple of his mates, I jumped into Niko's car and we drove to the television studios. Looking up, I stood amazed at the TV broadcasting tower, which at 275m high dominates the whole of Tbilisi from its perch on the 719m Mount Mtatsminda. "You like the tower?" he asked. "Then let's go up it!"

Chest out and with eyes gleaming, Niko looked proud as the four of us rattled up the rickety tower elevator. "The tower was built in 1974," he told me through one of his English-speaking colleagues, "but a massive fire completely burned out one section in 1992." Passing twisted metal and rusted walls, I could see the extent of the damage for myself. "We need several million dollars to mend it," Nicolai told me. "We really shouldn't stay up here for more than a few minutes, because the radioactivity is too intense." Just as he said this, the elevator ground to a sudden halt. We stood in pitch darkness, feeling the whole tower swaying and hearing it creaking in the howling wind. Managing to force the doors open a little, we shouted down to one of the workers far below. Carefully obeying the instructions that came in response, we squeezed out of the lift and groped our way in total darkness up two metal rung ladders before emerging on the top platform, where the sun shone and the wind blew. We were surrounded by several massive satellite dishes.

The view from the top was magnificent, but after a few minutes we were advised (because of the health risks) to come down again. That was easier said than done, as once more the lift had broken down. For 30 minutes we freely drank a heady cocktail of view mixed with several more doses of radioactivity before repairs were completed and we were able to descend once more to the relative safety of life on ground level.

And then it was straight off to the concert. That is, Nana, I and the girls went; Nicolai and his cronies had vanished. Around here, some things blokes do and some things girls do. I did everything. As we watched from our front-row seats, the top Georgian singer (I'm really sorry, but his name escapes me) crooned his way through his songs, while his three hundred fans oozed their adoration. Afterwards he pushed aside crowds of well-wishers in order to shake hands with Nana, me and the girls. "You shall come to my celebration party," he declared with a gushing, if slightly effeminate, sweep of his lavishly blinged hand. I wish I could remember his name.

Nana knew everyone at the party. The wine, served in many Wedding-of-Cana-sized glass flagons, flowed freely for the next few hours. As did the toasts. And the dancing. I was toasted by strangers who vowed life-long friendship with me, and who then cracked up uncontrollably as I attempted a couple of Georgian dance moves. Niko and his mates returned and I found myself sitting next to the English-speaking Irakli Jeianashvili, an ex-Red Cross employee now working with the government decentralisation programme.

Now just a word here about traditional toasting in Georgia. Toasting might be a slightly quirky but relatively relaxed activity in the UK but, despite our two nations having a soft spot for the same St George – he who slayeth dragons - the UK this most definitely was not. There is tradition, class, structure, balance and finesse to a Georgian toast, the manners and rituals of which have to be taken *very* seriously. At every *supra* (formal dinner) a *tamada* (toastmaster) orchestrates up to 35 toasts, all of which, it would appear, evolve in a strict order.

Firstly we toast *being* together. Fair enough. Then we toast the *reason* for being together. At this point I realise that it's going to be a long evening. I pray that I might stay sober. Jesus might have once turned water into wine, but right now I needed Him to turn it back again. Then the hostess (or in this case, the restaurant) is toasted, followed by the guests – particularly the special, bewildered foreign guest who, after an indeterminate but nevertheless finely nuanced pause, is then supposed to seamlessly respond to the toast, wait till everyone else has drunk, then down his extremely large glass of wine in one go. Then toasts are proposed to children, parents, absent friends, friendship, peace, Georgia, women, and to the toastmaster. Finally, a toast is given to a safe journey home which, by this time, and given the amount of wine that has been consumed, takes a considerable degree of faith.

Tonight the toastmaster is none other than my English-speaking friend Irakli who, because of this prestigious appointment, becomes a little too preoccupied to inform me of exactly what is happening. But not *too* preoccupied to give me a good twenty seconds warning in broken English, and a wine-induced slur, that it was now my turn to propose a toast. The toast was to Georgian women. At least, I *think* he said it was to Georgian women. I made full use of my twenty seconds, dutifully and carefully preparing my speech, but also fighting back an increasingly nauseating thought that he might well have said that the toast was to Georgian *chickens*. Finding simultaneous and complimentary things to say about women *and* poultry in my virgin toast at the 60th birthday party of a Georgian superstar was a challenge. With around nine seconds to go, I decided to risk it. The focus of my toast would definitely be to Georgian women. But not having a clue what Georgian women (or more significantly their large, increasingly drunk and warrior-like husbands) found to be particularly complimentary, I still had to admit that I really wasn't 100% sure of the best way to honour Georgian women. Tell you what. Strike a couple of noughts off that percentage. Not for the first time this weekend, I had not got a clue.

Very late that night, as we veered our way home, Natia listed my schedule for tomorrow. It was all sorted! And I arrived home to find all my clothes washed and ironed. What hospitality! What fulfilment! What answered prayer! I had drunk huge amounts of alcohol without getting drunk, danced (believe me, I *never* dance) and toasted Georgian women, all without causing an international incident between our two great nations. Of course, there is just a chance that these days in the market places, the good people of Tbilisi still continue to reminisce of the day when a skinny foreigner in muddy cargo trousers and two left feet spoke with such sincerity of the beauty, the grace and the femininity of the poultry of the southern Caucasus.

Sunday 9 May 2004

My adopted family indulged in a slower start the next morning, so I stayed in my room and wrote up some notes. However, despite her hangover (which for some reason I'm sure she said was making her feel like a toasted chicken) Nana was soon putting the finishing touches to our itinerary. While her husband remained on the town for the second consecutive night, we shared an almost silent breakfast together; me, her, and a Georgian/English dictionary. "I want to show you an orphanage," she said. Maybe my adoption was coming to an end. We bought a load of sweets and visited Street Children Rehabilitation Centre Momavlis Sakhli, 'The House of Future' for 6-18-year-olds in Tbilisi, spending some time with the children and listening to an impromptu concert of their songs. They pleaded for OCC gifts again next Christmas.

We shared a quick lunch with several of last night's diners. For 'quick lunch' read loads more food, vodka and toasts, but not the full set this time.

"Now we will go to Mtskheta," I was enthusiastically informed by young Tigger. Mtskheta is about twenty kilometres north of Tbilisi, in Kartli Region, at the confluence of the Mt'k'vari (Kura) and Aragvi Rivers. Steeped in history and having been declared a UNESCO World Heritage Site in 1994, Mtskheta was the capital of the ancient Georgian Kingdom of Iberia, where Christianity was proclaimed the state religion in 317AD. It is still the headquarters of the Georgian Orthodox and Apostolic Church.

Nana and her girls imploded into revered and head-covered silence as we looked round the Svetitskhoveli Cathedral (known as the burial site of Christ's mantle – described as 'a legend' according to Lonely Planet, but as 'an undisputed fact' by the guide), before clambering up the hill to the Jvari Monastery. This place was amazing. I wished I'd done more homework before coming.

I could hardly believe my ears when I heard we had a free evening ahead. What would I like to do? Well I may not have adequately researched the resting place of Christ's mantle, but I'd done *enough* homework to realise that at 6.00pm Dynamo Tbilisi were playing against their local rivals from Tbilisi, and a quick call to my old friend Irakli Jeianashvili resulted in him gathering together about a dozen friends and we all went off, some of them for the first time, to the football. Dynamo won this Umaglesi (Premier) League game 2-0, during which we were soaked in a sudden downpour. We did a slight detour on the way home so that Tia, one of the girls who came to the match with us, and whose uncle just happened to own the Kindzmarauli wine-making company, could gift me with six bottles of plush red wine.

Monday 10 May 2004

So that was it - my simple, low-key, in-transit weekend. I had packed and was ready to move on, with another silent five-hour car journey once more ahead of me, this time by taxi, across another border, to my tenth country.

Or so I thought. But there were just a couple of final people Nana wanted me to meet before I left. The girls had returned to their studies and Niko to his TV studios, so it was back in the Red Cross chauffeur-driven car for me and Nana. Another Red Cross colleague was dragged along as well, his role to speak a little English with the foreigner.

For our first meeting we drove across the city, arriving at the ornate palace of none other than Ilia II, His Holiness Catholicos Patriarch; head of the Georgian Orthodox Church. Nana thought that he would be interested in the work of Samaritan's Purse and, unbeknown to me, had arranged the meeting. I tried in vain to work out *why* he would want to see me, and what I should do, or say, exactly where I should kiss him or how I should address him, all of which was far too much for my translator. I think he understood my *questions*. He just had no idea of the *answers*.

We waited for a few minutes until summoned, and when Ilia II's security permitted us, we walked towards his huge and ornate office. There was nothing for it but to follow Nana, the determined and purposeful Head of the Georgian Red Cross Society, into the presence of His Holiness. In a split second of decisiveness, and as we walked through the door, I concluded in my wisdom that I would just copy whatever she did when greeting him. No sooner had I determined my strategy when Nana half curtsied, which despite the breadth of my by now famous cargo trousers made my 'do whatever Nana does' approach look a trifle ridiculous. He held out his hand to me, I held it, bowed slightly, and retreated to my chair.

I think the meeting went well, but it could have probably gone even better had I the foggiest clue what I was there for. However, His Holiness expressed a gracious interest in the work of Samaritan's Purse, and thanked me for our work with the vulnerable children of the world. Within fifteen minutes we had said our farewells, gone through security once more, and I relaxed into the back seat of the Red Cross car.

"For our last visit I want you to meet the President's father," said Nana from the front seat. Nothing surprised me anymore. President Mikheil Saakashvili was born in Tbilisi to a Georgian intelligentsia family. His mother was a historian who lectured at Tbilisi State University, and his father, Nikoloz, was a physician who practised medicine in Tbilisi and was the General Director at a local Balneological Centre. Now forgive me, but up until mid-morning on that Monday 10 May 2004 I'd never even heard of a Balneological Centre. But, it turns out, Tbilisi was built on a spring, and these days, surrounding that spring is the Balneological Centre. From the Latin *Balneum*, meaning bath, balneotherapy is the treatment of disease by bathing. The President's father greeted us warmly and showed us round the centre, where some people were bathing in the mineral-rich spa waters and others were receiving fangotherapy (the use of medicinal clays). Later, in his office, Mr Saakashvili senior explained how he wanted Samaritan's Purse to consider supporting the centre with a grant.

Then home for lunch. And that was it. Really, that was it. I didn't meet any other dignitaries. Not one. I jumped in a taxi and headed south, not knowing how best to thank my amazing hosts. Despite getting caught by a customs guard taking a photo at the border (he demanded I delete it, and watched over me while I did, then let me go), I made it into Armenia, and another entirely different adventure. But I won't ever forget the weekend when I transited through Tbilisi, sharing meetings, concerts, banquets, conference platforms and football matches with national leaders from NGOs, government, the arts, media, health authorities and the church. I was just beginning to understand the potential and influence of the job I had recently taken on. And I reflected sadly on the thinness of UK hospitality.

CHAPTER NINE

TSUNAMI

One of the greatest challenges I faced, both as an employee of Samaritan's Purse, and for my own emotional health, occurred in December 2004. Being the first Christmas I was to spend since my wife had left me, I had planned it out a bit in advance. I stayed with my second son Ben, and his wife, Tope, in London on the night of 24 December, and stayed over Christmas night with Joel and Ella in their (then) home in Brighton. As I jumped into the car on the morning of 26 December to drive up for the final part of my cunning plan of the holiday season - the Millwall v Ipswich football match at The New Den - I stabbed the radio button on, and knew instantly that something massive had happened. You could somehow tell just by the tone of the presenter's voice.

Few details were so far forthcoming, but they were suggesting that a Tsunami in Asia had resulted in at least 400 casualties. "Oh my goodness! Dear God," I groaned out loud; for I knew there was no way that such an occurrence would result in that small a number of casualties. The day continued, and the tragedy unfolded. I hardly remember the match. My heart was so heavy. I just wanted to get home and make contact with my friend of more than 20 years, Pastor Sanna Rajapakse, whose New Life Church serves the Tamil and Singhalese community in Kotahena, Colombo, Sri Lanka. It was to him that I'd sent doctors from Praise Community Church 14 years previously.

Sanna was out of town, and it wasn't until Monday 27 that I was able to contact him. He wasn't surprised that I'd called; he had already drafted a proposal for sending urgent dry food rations to some of the coastal areas affected. He had a network of pastors around the coast and the logistical contacts in Colombo to make it happen. All he needed was the cash. I informed my senior colleagues in Samaritan's Purse of my friendship with Sanna, what he had proposed, and an outline of his capacity to work with us on a larger scale. Within hours the word came back. Go to Sri Lanka as soon as possible. Later I was told by Dr Paul Chiles, consultant for Samaritan's Purse, that in 20 years of disaster relief, never before had he seen the local church be so immediately active in responding to a disaster.

By this time I had worked with Samaritan's Purse for 10 months and, although I had pursued a passion for supporting marginalised nations, communities, churches and peoples for more than 20 years, I felt utterly inexperienced at providing an immediate response to a major disaster. I'm normally the most level of people emotionally, but my time in Sri Lanka stretched me enormously, and exposed all kinds of frailties in my character and personality. The need for action was so urgent, and yet the longer-term task of redevelopment - through consultation with the local community – was so important to get right. The components of this dichotomy were constantly held in tension as, together with colleagues from around the world, I sought to formulate a strategic response to this massive disaster.

The 24 hours between being asked to go, and arriving at Heathrow airport to beg a place on the next flight, were possibly the most hectic of my life. I'm naturally a detail person who likes to make decisions carefully rather than quickly. I don't multitask very well (well I am bloke, so what do you expect?) and I like to methodically tick things off checklists. Everyone tells me how organised I am. If only they knew! Trying to complete plans for emergency relief during an extended Christmas Bank Holiday weekend was an interesting challenge. But I arrived in Sri Lanka on 29 December, armed with enough clothes and malaria tablets to last at least a couple of weeks. However, as things worked out, I was to stay for five weeks – surprisingly, the longest period of time I have ever remained outside the UK.

The next three days were hugely frustrating. Sri Lanka, as a diverse nation celebrates various ethnic and religious festivals and special days, resulting in something like 52 bank holidays. Inevitably New Year was yet another opportunity to close down offices and stores, thus making the purchase of urgent supplies extremely challenging. In Colombo, I did what I could to assess some of the immediate needs and arrange a response that matched the exponential growth of funds that donors were sending us. With all the stores closed again on Sunday 2 January, I was eager to see some action, and arranged for Sanna to take me to meet some of the survivors of the Tsunami.

We drove down the Galle Road on the west coast from Colombo to Hikkaduwa. Wherever the road went within 200 metres of the sea, everything was wrecked. Mile after mile after mile of devastation. Huge piles of debris were stacked on either side of the road (which was still closed south of Hikkaduwa), the railway line was utterly twisted and wrenched several metres from its bedding, and clusters of people stood by the sides of the road, hoping against hope that the endless stream of passing relief vans would stop and give them food, clothing or other essential supplies.

We stopped and spoke with a few families. Concy Wickramasinghe stood on the concrete base that eight days previously had been her attractive home, 100 metres from the coast in Kosgada. Not even one course of bricks remained. She was happy to talk, and welcomed me and Sanna onto her concrete base. I slowly became aware, from the porcelain-framed hole in the floor, that we were standing in what had been the toilet. Concy politely told me how she had held on tightly to her 80-year-old grandmother as the Tsunami swept them inland. She had been dressed in her Sunday best on the morning the disaster hit. One week later she was still wearing her Sunday best. These were her only clothes now.

Another man was loading what he could salvage from his property into a van. He showed me the remains of his possessions. A fax machine clogged with mud – I was quite sure it would never function again. He rubbed more mud off a picture frame. The wedding photo of his son and daughter-in-law slowly emerged. He looked at it so poignantly; I just didn't like to ask.

We drove on further. Substantial concrete buildings, built 100 metres inland, had been smashed to pieces by the impact of the sand and rubble in the wave, and grubby green lines high up on the few surviving walls marked the level the water had reached. Large vehicles were squashed; huge lumps of concrete and rooted trees had travelled distances to land wherever they willed. Large fishing vessels perched precariously on inland railway lines and orchards, where no self-respecting boat should be seen. Tangled fishing nets were strewn everywhere. Palm trees were withering due to the invasion of the salt water. The informally housed (shanty) communities did not stand a chance. All that was left of them were piles of wood fragments and twisted zinc sheets, with their contents - the occasional book or tee shirt or photograph - lying sodden or flapping in the breeze.

And all the while the gentle waves of the ocean rolled in; calm, idyllic.

On the following day we managed, through Samaritan's Purse UK funding, to purchase emergency aid packages for delivery to 500 displaced families on the east coast. Half the load was destined for Mullaitivu, the other half to Batticaloa. I accompanied the loads as they made their journey to the north east.

Having loaded our first two 10-ton trucks throughout Monday night, we set off from Colombo at six o'clock on Tuesday morning. It took more than 15 hours to drive to Mullaitivu, the northern city where we were to distribute our first load. This was the High Security zone, managed by the Tamil Tigers, or LTTE. It was a day full of checkpoints and uniforms and suspicious-looking lads with rifles. The further north we went, the worse the road surface became, and the little houses were increasingly made of mud and thatch. By the sides of the road were warnings of unexploded mines, and the remains of houses bombed in the civil war.

Arriving well into the evening, we (16 Sri Lankans and I) slept on the concrete floor of a church building, and were up at 4.30am to prepare for the remainder of the journey. The 16 Sri Lankans watched absolutely everything I did in amused fascination and delight. How this massively tall, thin, white-skinned man used a torch to see his way around, how he struggled to eat rice and curry using his right hand (I'm left handed), how he tried to communicate using an utterly foreign language, how he struggled to tie his sarong (that they insisted I wore), how he sat cross-legged on the floor (and still appeared to be a full head taller than them), how he tried in vain to wash modestly at an open well, how he shaved with a battery shaver, how he had to wear his socks and shoes because he was nowhere near being able to fit into the biggest flip flops they could find for him.

So on to Mullaitivu where, with Pastor Lesley Matthews from Jaffna, I distributed our load and met some of the local people. Here I met Kida Raj, the pastor of My Saviour Church, together with about 10 men, three women, and a handful of children from his church. "I was preaching whilst facing the sea," he told me, "and I saw the massive wave rolling in. I screamed to my congregation to run inland, and jumped on my motorbike to join them as we fled from the wave. But it soon overtook me and I had to swim for my life. Us men are all fishermen and can swim, but our wives and children couldn't."

Fifty-three of his congregation died, including his wife and children. Most of the men, and nearly all the women and children, perished. The survivors had lost everything, and looked utterly defeated. Apparently they had cried for 10 days and were cried out, but they still appeared dazed and in deep shock. These are simple uneducated people who cannot begin to comprehend why the Tsunami came, and who have no concept of the extent of the devastation throughout the region. They are used to being at the bottom of the pile; fishing was their simple life. Pastor Lesley Matthews and I prayed with these broken believers, shared simple Bible verses with them, hugged and held on and wept on their shoulders. Friends of Lesley had donated some monetary gifts for their essential needs that week. Stepping over the remains of Kida Raj's twisted motorbike, we left them sitting with drooped shoulders on the steps of their temporary home. Turning and waving goodbye seemed so ludicrously fickle.

Having completed my needs-assessment in the city of Mullaitivu and its surrounding villages (What city? What villages? They are utterly flattened) I drove another four hours back down-country where I was invited to sleep on another church-hall floor.

My second night sleeping on a reed mat on a concrete floor was no more comfortable than the first. But at least this time it was in relative privacy. There were only a mere twelve staring Sri Lankans that night, and hey, by now I was becoming pretty experienced at handling rice, curry and sarongs.

We were up again at 3.30am, as we had seven hours of driving to reach the refugee camp near Batticaloa, where the second distribution was due to take place. I was to meet Pastor Sanna there by midday. The journey took us through a section of jungle, where we cautiously shared the road with exotic birds, wild elephants, monkeys, mongooses, wolves and weird-looking boars with long snouts. In the weeks to come, a colleague driving this road was to have his pick-up truck rammed by an angry bull elephant, but no such drama today. Our two-vehicle convoy arrived in Batticaloa by midday. The two big wooden-framed trucks had come directly from Colombo with Sanna. On them were 250 packages each consisting of bottled water, two sleeping mats, a pillow, women and children's clothes, a sarong, a bucket, a kerosene lamp, a kerosene stove and some cooking utensils.

Sanna had delayed the distribution to await my arrival. I was grateful for this - for without witnessing the distribution I would have had no story to tell; and without a story, fewer donors would fund our programmes. But yes, I also felt the gnawing guilt of keeping nearly 400 shattered families waiting so that I could witness their suffering. However, waiting is what they have become good at. They are experienced waiters.

The refugee camp was based at Kirimichodai GTM School. I fully expected the camp to be maybe a mile or two out of the city, but this school was *way* out in the bush, about 20 kilometres off the main road, at the end a dirt track that our two trucks and people-carriers struggled to negotiate. A wild elephant grazed nearby. I found myself idly wondering if any elephants were washed away by the Tsunami. The school's usual function was to teach the children from the primitive villages in the surrounding area (I could see occasional mud and thatched houses randomly peeping out over the long grass), but it had no toilet. Even out here, one of the three local wells was saline from the impact of the Tsunami. The camp used one well, from which they drew and stored water in a tank on the site. The intention was to disperse the camp by the delayed start of term on 20 January.

Although we were asked by the authorities to go to this camp as one of three temporary settlements to distribute our aid, the closing of a few smaller camps over the previous 48 hours had caused this one to swell rapidly. There were now 1,901 people (385 families) living here, some of them actually sleeping in the school, some under UNHCR plastic, and the rest under trees or out in the open. Their toilet was the bush. Sixty-three of the families had lost a total of 85 members in the Tsunami. One hundred families had lost everything they owned. We had taken our carefully constructed parcels for 250 families but, because of the unplanned increase in numbers, we had to set up an enclosed area and hastily split 150 of the parcels into 300 smaller packages. The 100 families that had lost everything were still given a complete package. The other 285 families received a split (half) package, and the remaining few packages we later gave to families in the much smaller camp at Valaichenai.

Accompanying Sanna, and keeping him busy prior to my arrival, was a UK-funded mobile clinic (two doctors and seven nurses) that, whilst in Batticaloa, saw over 500 patients in two days. Had a hospital been available, only a few of their patients would have needed it, as there were no major disease outbreaks, but many had bronchial problems or untreated injuries, wounds and other strange diseases attributed to the Tsunami. Bizarrely, when I woke the following morning, I had about 50 glaring red spots decorating my forehead, and the morning after that I awoke to find that every one of them had completely vanished.

Before my trip to the north, experienced Sri Lankan aid workers in Colombo had stressed to me how I must be diligently careful about anything that even touched my lips, as there were some very unusual water-borne diseases breaking out in the camps. But in practice, the only place to clean one's hands (which became filthy again within minutes) was with contaminated well-water. And for cultural reasons, all the food that was available (mainly rice and curry) had to be eaten with the right hand. I ate very little all week, and slept even less. Apart from the two nights on church floors, another was spent packing the trucks and a fourth driving across the country - we left Batticaloa at midnight for our final seven-hour drive back to Colombo. Knowing that more missionaries die in car crashes than any other way, and having witnessed our driver work constantly for the previous 36 hours, I was terrified that he would fall asleep at the wheel. Many of the Sri Lankan aid workers and Christian volunteers I worked with had been living that way constantly for two weeks.

On Sunday 16 January, three weeks after the Tsunami hit Sri Lanka's beautiful coastline, I was back in Batticaloa and Ampara Districts on the east coast, where the Samaritan's Purse team was planning its medium and long term response to the disaster. I spent that weekend listening to more church leaders tell their stories of that dreadful day.

I met with Steve, a pastor originally from USA who lives with his Sri Lankan wife in Kottaikallar, near Kalmunai. His responsibilities included the oversight of several orphanages and two churches. When the first wave hit, people rushed into the church service he was leading to tell of what had happened. Steve ran to the beach to help the affected families just as the second (and massive) wave rolled in. He pointed to huge palm trees on the beach, and spoke with feeling of how the wave had totally enveloped them. "It was *the* most frightening thing. I never ever want to live through that again." That day his colleague, Pastor Vejay Kumarat, was presiding over another church service in the next village down the coast. The church building had just been completed, and had hosted its inaugural meeting on the previous day (Christmas Day). So their first-ever Sunday service had just begun when the Tsunami hit. Together with three attending members of his congregation, Vejay and his wife survived. Twenty died, including Vejay's 18-month-old daughter. Not untypically for a Sri Lankan congregation, up to 50% of the church members were late arriving, and consequently survived. Stories like this were repeated all around Sri Lanka's coastline. Many municipal offices and schools were destroyed but, being Sunday, not many people were working or studying. But many were attending church.

I heard of pastors who said they could not pray anymore, and of believers who just could not face attending church. Equally, I have also heard of numerous people accepting Christ as a result of the Tsunami, having called out for God to save them as the wave bore down upon them. These survivors subsequently confirmed their faith in Christ, and many were baptised.

Pastor Dayalan Sanders leads the Refugee Relief and Gospel Mission in Navaladi, Batticaloa. He is a dynamic leader, who week by week preaches a strong, Bible-based message of faith to his congregation. His church and its orphanage are situated at the far end of the idyllic 5km sand spit between the Indian Ocean and the Batticaloa lagoon. The complex is 300 metres from the sea shore on one side, and 50 metres from the lagoon on the other. This morning, together with a CBN film crew, I was invited with a couple of my Samaritan's Purse colleagues to be the first foreigners to join with them since the fateful day.

Pastor Dayalan told us his story. On Christmas Day they had celebrated with a big party for the local village children, and all who had attended had asked Jesus to be their Saviour. The children were given OCC shoebox gifts, and sent home on what for many was to be their final night. The party didn't end till after 10pm and, though his normal practice was to walk around the complex at the end of each day to pray and ensure the site was secure, the exhausted pastor decided to go straight to bed that night. Had he performed his usual routines, he would have detached and stored away the outboard motor from the 16-foot boat they typically used to shortcut across the lagoon to the mainland.

Next morning, at 8.50am on 26 December, Dayalan saw the terrifying sight of the Tsunami wave sweeping in. It dwarfed the elegant tall palm trees, and he said, "Roared like the sound of a thousand trains". He screamed to the children and adults on the site to get into the boat immediately, which was moored, outboard motor intact, by the edge of the lagoon. He then screamed again, this time at the wave, rebuking it and commanding it to be still in the name of Jesus. He slightly misquoted a Bible verse from the book of Isaiah that nevertheless came to his mind. "When the enemy shall come in like a flood, the Spirit of the Lord will lift up a standard against him."

The pastor described to me how the gigantic wave reared above their heads, angrily fighting to surge forward, but was somehow visibly restrained by an invisible force. "It was not just the size of it," he said. "It was evil, and raged at us furiously whilst at the same time being held back." But this invisible restraint gave enough seconds for all 32 people on the site to fling themselves onto the 16-foot boat. Unusually, the 15HP outboard motor – inadvertently still attached to the boat and ready for action - started first time, and they fled across the lagoon. As the wave was about to catch them up, Dayalan decided to spin the boat round and face the wave head on. Once more calling on the name of Jesus, they rode up the wave at an acute angle and, although being tossed around all over the boat, not one of those on board was lost.

The community on this exotic finger of land numbered five hundred families. Those villagers who survived now stay at a nearby refugee camp. The church and orphanage were the last buildings at the very end of the peninsular. One house in the village remained semi-habitable (every other one was utterly wiped out), and although half the orphanage complex was flattened, several more of the orphanage properties and the church building were virtually untouched.

The first orphanage boy to have seen the Tsunami shimmied up a concrete telegraph pole, and clung on tight while the wave powered over and past him. As I walked through what *was* the village this morning, virtually all the twenty or so concrete telegraph posts were smashed and strewn across the ground. In fact, the only two to stand upright were those in the orphanage complex. It was up one of these that the boy had climbed.

While I spoke tenderly with the congregation that morning, Dayalan interpreted, using a large Tamil Bible which was totally wrinkled on every page, but readable. Later he told me about it. By 12.30pm on the day of Tsunami, he had returned to survey the damage and to bury bodies of the villagers. He had begged the Lord that even if he had lost every one of his possessions, could he at least find his Bible? He found it lying utterly sodden, but readable and open at Isaiah 61.

> The Spirit of the Sovereign LORD is on me, because the LORD has anointed me to proclaim good news to the poor. He has sent me to bind up the broken-hearted, to proclaim freedom for the captives and release from darkness for the prisoners, to proclaim the year of the LORD's favour... They will rebuild the ancient ruins, and restore the places long devastated; they will renew the ruined cities that have been devastated for generations. Isaiah 61:1-2, 4 (NIVUK).

Dayalan remained in determined faith that God had anointed him to do just that, and that this community would be raised up 'as a planting of the Lord, that *He* may be glorified'.

95

One month on from 26 December, a few families were coming back to set up makeshift temporary shelters on the site of their destroyed homes. But people were still nervous about returning to the Tsunami-hit areas, and I saw a clear example of their anxiety one morning. I was back on the far tip of the Navaladi Peninsular, discussing with Pastor Dayalan the rebuilding of the Samaritan Orphanage. The cell phone rang. "Get off the peninsular immediately. There's word of another Tsunami approaching."

My first thought was sceptical. There had been rumours before. Why should this one be any different? But this time we were told it was official, and urgent calls to evacuate were being announced on the radio, so we jumped back into our 4 x 4 truck. The December Tsunami had utterly destroyed the road, limiting means of access to either taking a boat across the lagoon, or driving by 4 x 4 along the beach. That morning we had travelled by 4 x 4 and, on the way out onto the peninsular, the driver, very protective of his vehicle, had cautiously picked his way along the beach to the orphanage site. However, after receiving the phone call, the driver made the return journey at record speed. He jabbered away in high-pitched Sinhalese, and the word Tsunami came into every sentence.

On our tense way back to the mainland we were stopped by a gaggle of anxious youths. Could they use our phone? They desperately sought confirmation of the rumour, but all the lines they tried were engaged. By the time we made it back to the main road, fifteen minutes later, people were running to catch and squeeze onto buses; others were loading all their clothes onto trucks. There is one main bridge across the lagoon into the town of Batticaloa from the south. It was gridlocked. Pedestrians, bikes, motorbikes, trishaws, vans and buses all argued for access to the narrow bridge from both directions. As people made it out of the bush and onto the bridge we noticed that every person - whether they were driving, riding on buses or bikes – almost involuntarily looked across at right angles towards the sea. The gripping fear of another massive wave was consuming their terrified minds.

We made it to the town, where people cycled with determination and aggression, and motorbike riders hooted their horns urgently as they roared this way and that. Heated arguments broke out at the crowded petrol station, where 40 customers thrust their rupees at the flustered attendant in a stricken attempt to be served next. Fuel was being hurriedly pumped and slopped into flimsy plastic water bottles.

Then clear word from the government came suddenly over the airwaves. Although there had indeed been another 5.7 earthquake in Sumatra, there was no evidence that it had disturbed the sea levels or caused a Tsunami. With a collective sigh of relief, the town of Batticaloa settled down quickly. Within 30 minutes the filling station was empty, cycles were ridden once more at their usual sedate pace, and men chewing betel once more hung around in aimless groups. But the rumour had scratched a surface, and revealed that the apparent stillness in Batticaloa was only skin deep. However unlikely a second Tsunami might have seemed to me, I guess no-one who had actually witnessed 15 metre waves would ever live without some fear of them returning.

CHAPTER TEN
FORMER SOVIET UNION

am often asked which my favourite country is. This is such a difficult question to answer, and the natural beauty of Bosnia, Costa Rica, Kyrgyzstan, Montenegro, Nepal, Rwanda and Sri Lanka all come gloriously to mind, as does the sheer and delightful otherness of Azerbaijan, Cambodia, India, Iraq, Moldova and Sark. But probably even more than the scenery or the novelty, that covenant gene deep in my value system leads me to conclude that it's who you meet that has the biggest impact.

It was this staggering richness of relationship that so helped form and strengthen my sense of calling to Nicaragua, a country to which I have not managed to return since working with Samaritan's Purse. The countries I have returned to again and again, fostering valued friendship and partnership, include Azerbaijan, Belarus, Kyrgyzstan and Ukraine. I've made more than 75 visits to these four countries alone. Of course, these are four of the 15 countries that once collectively formed the Soviet Union. Those significant pre-Samaritan's Purse visits I had previously made to Nicaragua (during the Soviet-backed Sandinista era), and to Romania (immediately after the 1989 revolution), and to cycle across Russia, and to build houses in Kyrgyzstan, all gave me a deep passion for and commitment to Eastern Europe and the former Soviet Union countries.

Why do I love the countries of the former Soviet Union so much? After all, they are complex, corrupt, frustrating, environmentally disastrous, and exceptionally difficult to work in. After a generation of international support given to the post-Soviet world, these days the transitional nations (for some will remain in this state for some time to come) have been all but abandoned by the international church and NGO community, whose attentions seem to have been diverted almost wholesale into Asia and Africa, albeit in a reasonable attempt to meet firstly the UN Millennium Goals and then more recently the UN Sustainable Development Goals.

Nevertheless, as I see things, the majority of the transitional nations of the former Soviet empire still hang in a precarious and potentially explosive balance. Will they emerge as integrated, increasingly prosperous nations playing a vital and wholesome role on the world stage? Or will they separate themselves and become an alternative world power set up in opposition to others? Or will they descend into corrupt and unjust dictatorships, or into unmanageable, radical, extremist tribal groups without respect for or accountability to global society? Despite my prayers to the contrary, and while the global community abandons them to their uncertain future (or, worse still, feels threatened and dismissive towards them and blames them for all the planet's ills), I do fear for the future of this sixth of the world.

Once, whilst attending some meetings in Samaritan's Purse International Headquarters in Boone, North Carolina, some of my colleagues and I had the great honour of meeting an extremely high-ranking US government advisor on global defence trends. He delivered an amazing lecture on current global affairs, speaking with great eloquence and clarity, and giving us an extraordinarily convincing rationale as to why the particular hot spots of the time were kicking off, and which were the ones that were most crucial. Within this overview, he spoke of various key powers and potential super powers, their culture, their history and the interaction between them. It was one of those times when I wondered how on earth I could have possibly been included in such a privileged environment. When discussing present-day difficulties in Iran, he gave great respect to the historic Persian culture. He did the same with Israel and the Jewish culture and, with a little reluctance, to China and the Chinese culture. He even grudgingly acknowledged respect for certain aspects of ISIS; its passion and strategies. Then his tone changed as he said, "And then there's Russia." He puffed his breath out in distain and, arching his shoulders, spread out his hands in a show of utter dismissiveness. "Well, who on earth wants to be like the Soviet Union?" I couldn't believe it. In one sentence this eloquent global strategist, with direct and daily access to the (then) President of the USA, turned into what seemed to me like a threatened 14-year-old schoolboy talking defensively about the boy next door. "My President is bigger than your President." I was so discouraged. You can only poke the bear so many times. In the face of such an attitude, is it hardly surprising that the Russian government seek ways of reasserting themselves on the global stage?

However, I still haven't really answered *why* I love these former Soviet nations so much, and why I feel a sense of calling to that part of the world. And I'm not sure I *could* answer those questions adequately. That's why calling is a messy thing; emotional yet deeper than emotions. Calling needs to be of substance, justifiable and requiring accountability, but even when all these foundations are in place, calling somehow still leaks out at the sides. All I know is that, however frustrating and complex it is to work in this part of the world, I come alive when working there. Without trying hard, I constantly hold these nations in my thoughts and prayers and, however exhausting the trips, I was always ready for the next one.

Having persuaded my wonderful Belarusian friend and colleague Nicolai Balbutski to take me to see the magnificent Independence Day celebrations in Minsk, Belarus, I journaled my impressions.

> With the greatest of respect to the Dutch on their unexpected arrival onto Felixstowe beach in 1667, or to the French in Fishguard in 1797, and to the Germans in the Channel Islands in 1940, many claim that Britain has not been successfully invaded since the Norman Duke William II landed in Hastings in 1066.

> It is therefore difficult for us British citizens to understand what the big fuss is about when it comes to independence, self-rule, autonomy. In many ways we islanders sort of take it for granted.

> Not so in Belarus where, it seems, there has been no sanctuary from the constant yoke of external oppression, be it from the Lithuanians, the Poles, the Tsar, the French, the Bolsheviks, the Communist or the Nazis.

> But today is Independence Day: Sunday 3 July. No, this is not the anniversary of the day in 1991 when Belarus gained its independence from the former Soviet Union. In fact many around here regret that day. Today we celebrate the anniversary of the day when in 1944 Zhukov's Red Army completed the liberation of the country from the often barbaric Nazi occupation in the Great Patriotic War; a war in which two million people (almost 25% of the population) were murdered, some in concentration camps and others - men, women and children - simply locked into

100

buildings and burned alive. What on earth happens to the psyche of a nation that has suffered such grotesque and repeated, almost meaningless, injustice? Is it any wonder we Brits cannot begin to comprehend?

And so I ask to join the celebrations – to be a voyeur in another man's world. But first this morning Nic and I visit the Good News Baptist Church, neighbours to my landlords for the week - Andrei and Gala. After singing some old songs, witnessing the dedication of a baby, listening to the preacher and taking communion, we slip out and catch the Metro, which for a number of kilometres slithers efficiently right underneath Prospect Nyezhavisymosty – Independence Avenue.

Europe's cleanest and most ordered Metro system in Europe's cleanest and most ordered city was developed in the shape in a cross, and at the central junction we take the other line, north-west up to Nyemiga. It was on the steps of this Metro station that 53 people died in 1999, following a stampede to find shelter from a sudden torrential downpour at a free beer festival. Passing the spot where the 11th century origins of the city (1067, twelve months after the Normans landed in Hastings) are celebrated with a plaque, we walked briskly, and with hundreds of others, the one kilometre down Prospect Pobediteley (Avenue of Victors) towards the Stella – which itself celebrates victory in the Great Patriotic War.

Now during the last five weeks, the nation has been sorely troubled by an alarming economic collapse, and the panicked withdrawal by investors of almost all the hard currency from the banks. The exchange rate was around 3,500 Belarusian roubles per dollar a few weeks ago, and now it is anywhere between 5,000 (the official rate, but almost impossible to find) and 7,000. A small queue of people wait in an orderly line in most banks, in case anyone offers €uro or dollars in exchange for Belarusian roubles. The bank is legally obliged to exchange any hard currency they have, and thus, within seconds of me presenting my hard European currency for Belarusian roubles, one man had exchanged around 318,000 of his hard-earned roubles for my crisp new 50 €uro note. This collapse has effectively meant that pensions are worth half the value of a month ago, and we were told of one man with a serious disability who, of necessity, spends two-thirds of his pension on continence pads alone.

Protestors, rallied by social media, meet in Minsk each Wednesday and have adopted a tactic of slow hand clapping to show their concerns, not just about the economy but also about the way the country is run. Many arrests have been reported in the international media. So the President, in his speech on this Independence Day, claims that protestors are seeking to bring uncertainty and turbulence, but defiantly assures them that they will not bring Belarus to its knees.

Negotiating extremely robust security procedures (upon entering the cordoned-off area within 200 metres of the crossroads I am filmed, every item in my bag is investigated, my camera is turned off and on and off again, and I am made to drink from the water in my bottle) Nic and I arrive just as the tanks begin to rattle past. They create a thunderous roar on the suffering road surfaces. Thousands of people have gathered around the crucial junction of Prospects Pobediteley and Masherova, and we squeeze with determination into a place where we can watch the impressive military hardware rumble past. Only then do we realise that our proletarian vantage point is directly across the road from that of the President and his seven-year-old son Nikolai, who is being groomed for greatness and accompanies his father on many such ceremonial occasions these days.

After the tanks come the missile launchers. After the missile launchers, the helicopters and the planes fly overhead. After the helicopters and planes come the gymnasts, the athletes, the elite sportsmen and women, dancers, break-dancers, the Children of Octobriata (8-11's), Pioneers (12-15's) and Belarusian Republican Union of Youth (16-28's). All are accompanied by military bands and hundreds of red and green flags, and banners with slogans exalting a 'blossoming Belarus'. And at the end, as a gift for young Nikolai (who by his applause and the smile on his face seems more impressed with the break-dancers than the military hardware), thousands of red and green balloons are released into the sky. It is a wonderful atmosphere; truly majestic, magnificent, proud, bold, loud, festive, celebratory, exhilarating.

Nic tells me he has mixed feelings: understandable pride mixed with a realisation that this is actually just like the Soviet days, even down to the uniforms of the young Pioneers. But for all my trips to the former Soviet Union, I have never before witnessed a May Day or Independence Day parade, and I am transfixed. For 50 years I have dreamed of what it would be like to witness and to taste the atmosphere of such events, and here at last is one before my very eyes.

Nic eventually tears me away and we walk back through the Park, through the beautiful Troetskoe Predmestie - Old Town Minsk with its 19th century central European feel (it is one of the few areas not demolished by the Nazis in the Great Patriotic War). We eat lunch on a boat restaurant while it rains, and eventually we return on the Metro to the car.

Late that evening I walk out again, alone this time to watch the 11pm fireworks that wrap up the day's events, and I reflect on a magnificent day, and on what an honour it has been to take part in it. Yes, the rouble has collapsed; yes, the world is pressing its demands for conformity upon the nation's leadership, and yes, many are protesting for change. Cleary there are winners and there are losers. Yet as I stare into a darkened summer sky that sparkles colour tonight over a justifiably proud and independent nation - and one which knows how to celebrate this precious fact with glory, pomp and grandeur - with great affection and appreciation I pray. I pray for this nation, its leadership, its church and its people, that God will bless and protect it, and that the Kingdom will come, that the will of God will be done, in Belarus as it is in heaven.

But it is not only the rich and varied cultures within the former Soviet Union that I love. I also love its Church, and have rejoiced in the roles I have had to help it connect with its communities. This is probably better described as *reconnecting* with communities, for a particular and very understandable reason. For what happens to the psyche of a Church that has had to look nervously over its shoulder for seven decades of anti-religious communism? With some glorious exceptions, it tends to implode. It retreats into its shell – its meetings and its buildings. Its incarnational influence in its community weakens, and it settles for spending its time and energies on internal discussion and debate surrounding the trivia of theoretic and non-essential doctrines.

But after 70 years of communism, along came Gorbachev, *glasnost* and *perestroika*. Freedom and restructuring. There followed an explosion of Christian growth in the 1990s, when people's hunger for alternative ways of living was fresh and insatiable, and when it became trendy for Western missions to almost *throw* funds, often indiscriminately, at churches in the former Soviet countries. Then, following the millennium, there came a more sobering decade, when young independent governments had to contend with disillusionment, fundamentalism and the beginnings of an economic downturn. In these challenging days, in terms of persecution and of the economy, the indigenous church of Eastern Europe and Central Asia is seeking to grow up. It's now finding its own identity, and its own fresh connections with its communities and their rapidly transitioning culture.

At the same time, many Western mission agencies became bored, or frustrated with the culture. Others who came with more of a prosperity gospel, possibly became embarrassed when the shallowness and self-centredness of their approach became more evident. Large numbers of these missions stopped paying for huge church buildings to be constructed, ended their agreements to pay local pastors inflated salaries, and left. The foreign missionaries that remain in the region these days tend to be sincere, egalitarian servants, respectful of the culture and of the local church, and are working hard in genuine community-based programmes and initiatives that support, equip and enable rather than dominate and control.

CHAPTER ELEVEN
DISCOVERY TEAMS

n the years after I started working with Samaritan's Purse UK, the culture of the organisation developed considerably. I would describe the basic approach to our work when I joined in 2004 as being that of giving things to, and doing things for, the poor. It was a rather random (albeit strongly relational) approach, fuelled by who we knew and by what gave us and our donors some emotional satisfaction, rather than being underpinned by a strong sense of strategy or intelligent missiology.

Through the pain of much change, and under the skilful leadership of its Executive Director, and despite the inevitable move-on and appointment of different members of staff, gradually Samaritan's Purse developed a clear strategic approach with regard to the work it wanted to do, where it wanted to do it, and who it wanted do it with.

Increasingly it became known not only for its 'shoebox' programme, but also for its relief and development work. And although our office was tiny in comparison, we also began to work more closely with our huge International Headquarters in the US in the sending of specialist people to manage disaster (emergency) relief responses around the world. Our development sector specialisms included work with Orphans and Vulnerable Children (OVC), with clean water, sanitation and hygiene programmes (WaSH), with social protection (including HIV and AIDS responses), and with livelihoods.

Our geographical focus was now more clearly on Africa, Eastern Europe and Central Asia, although we would still go wherever in the world a major disaster occurred.

Whereas previously our partners included a random selection of NGOs, charities and agencies, some faith-based and some not, we were now becoming committed wherever possible to working with and through the local church, perceiving this to be God's main agent for the Kingdom of God on the earth.

We also continued to run our short-term mission team programme, annually sending between 15-20 teams of UK-based volunteers to work alongside our partners. This was an exciting but expensive and ultimately unsustainable programme, and involved sending many OCC distribution teams, work teams, and volunteers to serve in summer camps and soccer camps, mainly in Eastern Europe and the former Soviet countries, and then increasingly into Africa.

Although I *watched* a lot of football when I was young, I didn't *play* that much. I wasn't that good. OK, with a group of mates – when we were about 19 or 20 – we did enter a five-a-side league in Ipswich, and once even reached the heady heights of some semi-final or other, playing in front of 500 or so people. But then, bizarrely, and after 30 years of inactivity on the pitch, my silky skills were required once more. By now I was well into my 50s.

Before and at the time I joined Samaritan's Purse, they used to send ex-professional footballers to host fun soccer-coaching programmes in Eastern Europe and Africa. We would hire the national or another major stadium (in Moscow, Baku, Minsk etc), and invite the most marginalised of children to train and play on the pitch with ex-pros from such clubs as Liverpool, Everton, Birmingham City and Newcastle United. Manchester United and Ipswich Town also supported us by giving us kit to distribute to the children. In this way, street kids (whose previous moments of soccer fame had been limited to picking up plastic bottles outside the arena) were now playing on their hallowed turf with good footballers, even including a few ex-pros from the UK Premiership. At the end of the week we would put on an exhibition game against a local side. It's true, I only came on twice as a substitute, once in Monrovia (Liberia), and once, my final swansong, in Kiev (Ukraine). But oh, what a moment of glory! No word of a lie, we trounced none other than the Ukraine national football team, 3-0; the Ukraine girls' under-18s national football team, that is.

Operation Christmas Child distribution teams would go to some of the countries where the UK OCC gift-boxes were being distributed, this giving our faithful UK volunteers the opportunity of seeing 'the smile on the child's face'. They would come home and generate further interest in the programme by sharing their experiences. These OCC distribution trips were also an opportunity for us to introduce people to the complexities of the transitional world, and sometimes of what it was like to walk shoulder to shoulder with the persecuted church.

Such as the day our team was on the south shore of the second-highest lake in the world, in the foothills of the glorious, 'Celestial' Tien Shan Mountains that stretch across Western China into Central Asia. Our UK team of fourteen had grown to a convoy of 26, with film crew, local pastor, OCC National Leadership Team and interpreters. We had just slept fully-clothed (including coats, hats and gloves) in a bitterly cold and seemingly derelict Pioneer Camp, which continued to host families and groups at warmer times of the year. One of the team members had politely asked in which year the centre had closed.

But the sun on the snowy mountains soon warmed us to a new day and, as we headed east again, to a quiet and photogenic village where tiny wooden ginger-bread houses and slender silver birch trees lined a street littered with dogs, cattle, a pre-revolution Moskovitch car, and an ancient motorbike or two. It was Sunday, and one team member asked if we would be going to church. But we weren't sure if our hosts' plans included going to church.

We were destined for the village school, where a crowd of 60 or so people were gathered around the entrance. But rather than displaying the usual excitement that we had grown to anticipate upon the arrival of the foreigners, these villagers seemed subdued.

It transpired that the local authorities had forbidden the OCC distribution to go ahead. Whether it was due to the presence of foreigners, the Christian influence or just petty bureaucracy, we were never to find out. But a plan emerged. We would take the cartons that contained the shoeboxes from the school store and, whilst we kept our eyes peeled for officials, the distribution would take place in the deserted house that was now being used as the village church.

The men on the UK team went to the school store and naturally insisted that they (rather than the local women) carried the heavy shoebox cartons onto the trolley. One woman, middle-aged, wrapped in a big coat and scarf, and already flushed by the raw sun and snow, coloured up even more as she later told her friends, "I felt like a real woman today. They wouldn't let me lift the cartons." You could never tell when and how the incarnational love of Jesus would touch a person's life.

Immediately across the road from the mosque, the house-church had windows that had been smashed by antagonists. The believers in this village of 3,000 people numbered around 25, but possibly 250 people eventually climbed over the high threshold and through the little doorway that Sunday morning, and spilled out into the yard at the back, much to the bewilderment of the neighbour's goat.

And there took place the most wonderful Operation Christmas Child distribution. The children's leader sang songs and played games with the village children, and the UK team moved around expressing love and kindness to children and parents. We were only able to share a little of the redemption message we had come to bring, honouring the need for extreme sensitivity and respect for the on-going mission of this persecuted church. But the children loved their boxes, and afterwards, as the UK team drank tea from a samovar and prayed with the local believers before leaving for its next distribution, we realised we had definitely been to church.

- - - - -

In 2005 I was given a new role with Samaritan's Purse. As well as maintaining my existing role of building partnerships, I took on the management of our short-term teams programme, utilising my 20 years of experience of leading mission teams with Praise Community Church and Habitat for Humanity. I was keen to maintain what I saw as the best of the existing programme, and yet to develop its culture into a more reciprocal, partnership approach.

The plan was that we would still go and perform some *tasks* (after all, sadly we Westerners seem to be unable to find our identity or justify our existence unless we are fulfilling a task), but no longer would these tasks be the *reason* for such teams to be sent. I spent many hours with our management team, our team leaders, and our team members, persuading them to move from the deeply entrenched UK-centric mind-set of 'giving things to and doing things for poor people', promoting instead the value of relationship, of learning, and of longer-term partnerships. To be compatible with this change of emphasis, I renamed the programme Discovery Teams, and promoted two new strap lines. One was 'Short-Term Teams Serving Long-Term Goals' and the other was 'Hungry to Learn; Eager to Serve'. I would tell stories of how God did short-term mission, incarnationally, by sending His only Son to earth. And I would tell stories of how Jesus sent short-term teams, and how they were not sent only to fulfil a task, but also how the mission experience was an amazing means of equipping and maturing the disciples themselves for future service.

Missionaries, they say, are like prunes. They go into the dark interior and do good. The modern day missionary movement, pioneered by people like William Carey in the late 18th century, has been historically symbolised by a few faith-filled men and women who have sacrificed everything, spent a lot of time overcoming local opposition to their plans and, where possible, investing into lengthy training, before setting sail for dark and mysterious places unknown, rarely to be heard of again, and maybe taking half a century to plant a small church, or even no church. Many would never return, becoming victims of violence or disease. There is even a memorial to such a faith-filled pioneer in my own church building in Ipswich (a plaque commemorating the life and death of a missionary killed in the anti-Christian Boxer Rebellion in China in 1900), and the first pastor of the church where I was a pastor in Thrapston, Northamptonshire also had a major role in the sending of William Carey as the 'Father of modern missions' to India in 1792.

I clearly recall an elderly missioner speaking in the church I attended as a child with my parents. Focusing his eyes firmly on me, he worked up to the inevitable crescendo of a call for young people to give their lives for the mission field. Apart from me and my parents, the next youngest in his congregation must have been 83. "Is it me, Lord?" The old missionary obviously thought so.

Times have changed, of course, for better *and* for worse, but now the overseas mission trend is for flexible, shorter, contextualised training and shorter stints on what used to be called the mission field. And of course, many missionaries are coming *to* the UK these days, and in our globalised society, every believer needs some cross-cultural awareness if they are going to take the gospel even across the street.

For five years or so, at least 70% of my work with Samaritan's Purse was in the development of short-term mission teams, a phenomenon which has grown rapidly over the last couple of decades, and which gives people the opportunity to go for a couple of weeks and see for themselves a different culture, and to learn some good missiology by living, loving and working alongside the local church around the world.

Debates rage around the value of sending such teams. Good questions are asked, sometimes out of cynicism and misunderstanding, sometimes out of a genuine hunger to ensure that we stop messing up on the international stage and start getting it right. Why don't you just send them the money? Surely you just get in the way? Doesn't a team going and doing a task for local people just take their jobs from them, and build an unhealthy dependency on the West?

I have looked into all these issues deeply and honestly, as there is no simple answer to them. It depends a lot on context, expectations, attitudes, leadership and purpose. But for me, one absolutely fundamental aspect of a good short-term mission team remains constant throughout, and that is the value of connections, of relationship, of being, of incarnation. I wrote the following story to help those with a purely task-focussed approach to short-term mission teams to consider a fresh, more relational approach, through the greatest incarnational model we have ever had. It was called 'You Are Here'.

> The Father and Jesus were talking one day in heavenly places. Throughout the old covenant, the righteousness and faithfulness and compassion of God had been poured out from heaven onto the brokenness of humanity,
>
> - Sometimes by way of a God-given *leader* such as Abram, Moses or David.
> - Sometimes by way of a *miracle* breaking through from heaven, such as a burning bush, or the daily provision of manna, or the driving back of the sea.
> - Sometimes by way of God's *judgment*; maybe a disaster or a crisis such as a serious economic downturn to bring people back to their senses.
> - And sometimes by way of a *prophet*, who would speak the word of God without fear into rebellious and self-consumed communities.

But still mankind rebelled. So one day Jesus was talking with the Father, and voicing out loud the possible strategies that would be appropriate at this moment of time for the restoration of His people on earth. Should it be another leader, another disaster, another miracle, another prophet again this time?

But the Father had already turned and was gazing distantly out of the window. He became quiet - *very* quiet, deeply thoughtful, intensely troubled. Jesus stopped in mid-sentence, and quietly, expectantly, nervously watched His Father's back. *Speak* to me, He thought. Just *speak* to me. But the Father remained silent. Slowly, deeply, silently, the enormous truth dawned on Jesus, and eventually and with a cracked voice He quietly said to His Father, "It's *me*, isn't it? It's me. *I've* got to go, haven't I? This time I've actually got to *go*."

For the rest of the day the Father sat with Jesus and outlined His ultimate plan for the salvation of the world. Every few minutes new depths of awareness crashed into Jesus, Son of God, Lamb, Bread, Bridegroom, Shepherd, Cornerstone, Rock, Vine, Word, as the Father outlined what sort of birth He would have, what sort of life He would lead, what sort of death He would suffer, and why.

Incarnation. It's all about *being*. It's all about being *here*. And it's all about discovering and connecting with God's fingerprint. By coming to another culture you are entering into a conversation that is already happening.

So, mission is a matter of finding where God is already at work, and joining in. My friend Gordie Lagore told me once of a First Nations lady in northern Canada, and how she had greeted him when he arrived in her community with a short-term mission team. "If you think you have come to help us, you are wasting your time. But if you believe that somehow your healing is tied up with ours, then come and let's live and love and work together."

Another reasonable criticism of short-term teams is that they are a two-week sparkle that fizzles into history when the team returns to the UK. On the contrary, I am convinced that to be credible, short-term teams must serve long-term goals, not only with the host partners but also with team members. The short-term team is purely one small but exciting step in a lifetime journey of discipleship and development. I wrote this version of a famous story to outline how Jesus approached this issue. I called it 'Coming Home'.

Whilst on our short-term mission trips, we live an intense common-purse community lifestyle, and despite being well outside our comfort zones, we open ourselves up to the point of vulnerability, and give ourselves away in long hours of joyful self-sacrifice.

When we eventually arrive home, we are exhilarated yet exhausted, physically and emotionally. Subconsciously, maybe even consciously, it is easy to assume that everyone will understand that it's now *our* turn to be looked after for a while. When these silent presumptions and expectations become crystallised into demands of the heart, however, we can find ourselves in more than a spot of bother.

To be honest, life was probably *not* actually tougher when we were away on our trip. In fact, in a lot of ways, it was probably easier. Adrenaline was pumping; we were fuelled by intrigue, excitement. Everything was so new, so special, and faith levels were high. We were able to encourage and stimulate one another through the wonderful, open, grumble-free, collective team dynamic. Despite the poverty around us, we were well looked after, didn't have to cook or wash up, were treated like royalty, had an acutely heightened sense of identity and purpose, and virtually forgot about the distresses and debts, the discontents and difficulties that we had left behind at work and at home.

The first six verses of Luke chapter 9 tell us about the very first exciting short-term mission team experience of the twelve disciples. They give us an outline of their pre-trip training and orientation, their objectives, and how the team members were to respond to good times and to bad. These few verses even give us the team member packing list, right down to the number of shirts they were to take.

All sorts of things happened while the disciples travelled together, and God really turned up for them like never before. When it was time to come home, they couldn't wait to tell Jesus what had happened.

But they were in for a big shock, and for another immediate and intensive growth experience. For the moment they returned, they were greeted with news of a massive tragedy. John the Baptist had just been murdered - beheaded at the manipulated wish of Herodias' dancing daughter. Not only were the disciples utterly exhausted by their mission trip, but they were now in shock, completely deflated and full of fear. The euphoria and exuberance of their trip had been instantly swept away, completely lost in the blackness of this devastating news.

The wisest course of action seemed to be to withdraw, together with Jesus, and chill out for a while in Bethsaida. Here they could escape from life's interruptions. But as they left, and to their horror, a huge crowd followed them. This multitude seemed totally oblivious of the disciples' need for a bit of space and regrouping time.

When the crowd were still milling round late into the afternoon, the twelve decided that enough was enough. Along with the setting sun came a distinct chill in the air, and the disciples came to Jesus and told Him unequivocally to send the mob away. There was no food and no lodging, and the place was remote. There was a restlessness stirring in the crowd, as though they somehow blamed the *disciples* for bringing them so far out of town. Although this was *so* unjust, they could soon have a riot on their hands.

Jesus seemed totally unconcerned. Despite His intense grief over the violent end to the cousin He loved so much (to say nothing of what the disciples had perceived as the obvious priority need of Him giving *them* His time and attention for their mission team debrief and re-entry weekend), He had actually spent the whole day chatting easily with the crowd, and healing their sick. As John commented to no one in particular, "He just seems to have great compassion on them, as though they are sheep without a shepherd."

"I wish He had as much compassion for us," Thaddaeus muttered to Thomas. "We've flogged our guts out over the last few days. Surely He can see we're at the end of our tether?"

"If He thinks I'm going to give Him five out of five on the evaluation form for 'debrief and post-trip support' He's got another think coming," Thomas replied.

But actually, stretching time was about to begin once more, and the reality of what it means to walk constantly and obediently with Jesus was to hit them hard again that night. Exhausted as they were, they worked long and hard again all evening, and watched in bewilderment as it slowly became clear that five loaves and a couple of fish would prove too much food for the crowd of five thousand to eat.

Late that evening, with the crowd replete and eventually settled down, and the crickets doing what crickets do loudly in that part of the world at night, Peter threw another log on the camp fire and, with his friends, he reflected upon another miraculous, stretching, grieving, roller-coaster day. And they realised that they couldn't just turn responsibility on for the duration of an occasional highly-charged, public, short-term mission trip, but that the Master had called them to a 24/7 lifestyle of servanthood, be they at home or away. Of taking up their cross day by day by day, be they in the mood or not, and following Him.

It has been a great privilege to work with such a diverse cross section of volunteers from the UK and beyond, who commit to raising their own funds, learn what it means to be a team, and discover what God's Biblical mandate for cross-cultural mission is all about, and to lead them on their trip of a lifetime. Time and time again I have seen peoples' lives moulded, formed, influenced and even transformed by their short-term mission experience.

It slowly dawned on me that having had some direct leadership influence in at least 90 such short-term mission team programmes, over 30 years and in 30 different nations, I was probably one of the most experienced people in the UK in this sector. During this time I began to work closely with Global Connections, a best practice resource for UK-based mission agencies, and for several years served on their Short-Term Mission Team core group. As well as hosting an annual conference for the debate and development of short-term mission, we also manage a 'Code of Best Practice' process for those that send out short-term teams. At the time, over 40 UK-based mission agencies served under this Code.

CHAPTER TWELVE

BELA

I n 2005, I was still overseeing the management of OCC in the countries to which we sent the gift boxes. One such country was Azerbaijan. Our lead partner was Bela, who worked as a Special Projects Coordinator for a Christian NGO in the capital city, Baku.

One day Bela came to me, not on behalf of her organisation and OCC, but independently, to enquire as to whether Samaritan's Purse would consider sending a Discovery Team to help lead a summer camp for the children of her church. I agreed to consider this and, as we continued to discuss the details after my return to the UK, we realised our emails were becoming more friendly and personal. It transpired that Bela was a divorcee and mother of two, who had met with God through a powerful experience of the Holy Spirit in 1999. She loved God, loved her children, loved her job and loved her nation.

On my next visit to Baku, we talked openly about our tender but growing relationship, and naturally, warmly, innocently, sensed that God could well be drawing us together. The last thing on Bela's mind was to leave Baku, the city she loved and had lived in all her life. However, I suggested that she come to visit me in the UK, and during that time we could explore whether or not God was drawing us to lead the rest of our lives together. So Bela came to visit me. I introduced her to the sights of East Anglia - to Cambridge, to Constable Country, to Aldeburgh - and to London. We spent those days walking, talking and praying together, and by the end of the two weeks, we just couldn't imagine going our separate ways.

At the time, I knew nothing of the fact that Bela had specifically prayed to God for a 'light-haired, light-eyed believer man'. Such creatures are an almost unimaginable rarity in Baku, but Bela, having previously sensed that God had heard her prayer, was now being presented with God's answer. Later, when she told me this, I felt so relieved that she hadn't added 'young, good looking and rich' at the end of her list of requirements.

Baku is a wonderful city. It is classy, noble and sophisticated; colourful, hectic and dynamic; mysterious, historic and exotic. But sadly, and having lived in this environment all her life, Bela also knew as well as anyone just how deep the corruption that seeps into this society could be. Different people advise different routes to get the simplest of things done but, whichever route one chooses, it involves the giving of bribes. When my bride-to-be investigated the process of having us formally married in Baku, she concluded that the state had given it to one department, who had given it to one woman, to register all foreigners wanting to marry Azeri citizens in the country. This registrar would assess the situation (i.e. how rich is this person and the country they are coming from) before charging what she alone deemed to be an appropriate fee for the form that needed to be filled in. With the form completed and returned, she would then ask for more money for the next form, and so on. However, these were not referred to as bribes. They were called Respect. When Bela was waiting to speak with the registrar, she talked with a Turkish woman in the queue who said that she had returned to Azerbaijan three or four times to seek this marriage registration, and was still no nearer to achieving it. We therefore decided to wait until we were together in the UK before formally registering our marriage. This registrar was giving corruption a bad name.

We made our marriage vows at Bela's local church's Friday evening meeting in Baku, on 1 September 2006. None of my UK family or friends were present, and the service was in Russian. I said "I do", in Russian. I'm not entirely sure *what* I said I'd do, or how I'd do it, or when I'd said I'd do it by, but things seem to have turned out all right! Putting aside the 25 days when we had purely sat in business meetings together, we worked out that we'd only actually set eyes on one another for a total of 22 different days before we were married.

It was another five weeks before all their forms and logistics were sorted out, and on the day before her daughter, Nargiz's, 18th birthday Bela, Nargiz and Kamal (then almost 13) arrived in the UK. My home was empty no longer.

As Bela did not drive at the time, and I was travelling away from home so regularly, we decided to find a church within walking distance of our home. My finale at Earl Soham Baptist Church was the day our wedding vows were confirmed, and immediately afterwards we joined Burlington Baptist Church in Ipswich, which has been our spiritual home ever since.

Having grown and developed from a traditional Baptist Church under the leadership of Simon Harris, Burlington is publicly known these days for its strong teaching, its great music and worship, and its missional communities. However, behind the scenes a host of other missions and services are going on, for which we have great respect. Despite the random nature of our travelling lifestyle over the years, which has limited our involvement in much of the day-to-day life of the church fellowship, we are loved and accepted, and feel very much at home with this local church community.

It took the best part of five years to sort out all the paperwork (and pay all the ever-increasing fees) required to confirm Bela's 'indefinite leave to remain' in the UK, and then to establish her citizenship, and to secure the rights on her small apartment back in Baku, which was still registered as belonging to the state under the old Soviet system. During this time she also learned to drive, pursued an Open University course in Social Sciences and, more recently, a TEFL course. Bela became a self-employed sole trader doing translation and interpreting work, and has also worked and volunteered within a number of local government and social sector specialisms throughout East Anglia.

But possibly the most interesting employment opportunity opened up for her upon my return from yet another trip to Kyrgyzstan. While I was away, Bela had been told that the Azerbaijan National Olympic Committee had responded to an offer by Ipswich Borough Council, from their offices just across the river from our home, to use Ipswich as their 2012 pre-Olympic games training base. Upon hearing this, I instantly phoned the Council, asking them what they were doing about interpreting, translation and cultural awareness training for their staff. They confessed they were totally stuck, and were so delighted when I told them of the nationality and CV of my wife that they invited her for an interview that very afternoon. As a result, Bela worked as a consultant liaison officer both for Ipswich Borough Council, and also for University Campus Suffolk, developing partnerships between the town she now lives in and the nation she is from. After the Olympic Games this partnership evolved into the worlds of arts, culture and education, involving us attending prestigious red carpet events in London and in Baku, and holding regular meetings with Members of Parliament, Presidents and Vice-Presidents of Olympic Committees, Heads of Government Departments, and the Ambassadors of both countries.

Azerbaijan is a truly extraordinary country, with a magnificent wealth of scenery, culture and natural reserves. Strategically placed immediately to the south of Russia and to the north of Iran, it has huge oil and gas wealth from the Caspian Sea to the east, and desperately painful and unresolved issues in its relations with Armenia, its neighbour to the west. With a dominant Shia Muslim population, Azerbaijan's language and culture is of Turkic origin, and it declared independence from the collapsing Soviet Union in 1991. Is this Europe or is it Asia? This is a question that no one seems adequately able to answer. This is the Caucasus.

The occasional visitor (for this is all I can claim to be, despite my fifteen or so visits to all corners of the country, my marriage to an Azerbaijani citizen and my meetings with many senior government and Olympic officials) might easily recall Winston Churchill's famous assessment of Russia in 1939 and apply it to Azerbaijan today: 'a riddle wrapped in an enigma inside a mystery'.

If one journeys off the beaten track to explore the glorious mountains, woodlands, orchards and deserts, one discovers a mysterious and medieval culture of Khans and Kingdoms, of petroglyphs and palaces, of mosques and mausoleums, of carpets and caviar, and of villages and volcanoes. Yes, Azerbaijan is home to almost half of the world's 700 known mud volcanoes.

But many visitors arrive purely for business purposes, and never see beyond the extraordinary *nouveau riche* of the capital. Baku is a complex place. On one hand it is hugely confident, prosperous and cultured. Its Old City is magnificent. Its Maiden's Tower is unique. Yet hidden behind these riches, old and new, lie agonising stories caused by poverty, injustice and strife. It's not an easy city, but I love it, and sometimes I'm confused and not a little afraid by some aspects of its extraordinarily rapid transformation. Like the day I walked the Bulvar.

> Baku. It was a sunny, windy, Sunday afternoon in April when I walked along the *Bulvar* (promenade). Bakuvians in their hundreds idly promenaded, ambling carefree by the water's edge, as though this

particular day of the week somehow forced them to walk at half speed. Boys walked with boys, laughing and joking at the girls. Girls walked with girls, laughing and joking at the boys. Boy walked silently with girl, dignified, proud. Girl walked silently with boy, contented, smiling. Parents walked alert, attentive, ready to bring adjustment as their toddlers randomly explored the next flower, the next puddle, or the next bird to land near them. Three women in their fifties unashamedly voyeured, commented, gossiped from the bench on which they sat. And an old man hobbled, alone, very alone, bemused, watching with bewilderment and through large, thick, cracked spectacles the world that is changing unbelievably before his fading eyes.

And how rapidly his world is changing. And mine too, for I first visited Baku in ancient times, seven years ago. Not long after the Zoroastrians left, or so it feels now. Even in the two years since I was last here, many things have changed. For example, the highway between the airport and the city centre, which we drove down when arriving at six o'clock this morning, and where the eight lanes of grand and perfectly-smooth tarmac is these days bordered either side by six-metre high walls of marble and pale stone, carved with ornate, exotic, almost oriental decoration. Each section is illuminated - celebrated - with a dignity more typically reserved for Istanbul's Blue Mosque or Agra's Taj Mahal. But I've been here before, and I've seen what everyone used to see before the tarmac became smooth and the walls became high. Broken infrastructure, derelict factories, the desolate slurry of waste from the oil and gas industries, and crumbling mud-built houses with the customary abandoned Moskovitch left wheel-less and rusting in the courtyard outside. But these days, post-Zoroastrian, the first-time visitor, as he cruises along this tunnel of affluence, sees nothing but radiant marble.

And so it was with the Bulvar, or at least it will be by the time the façade is complete. Constructed of marble pillars linked by bright steel railings, it has a low wall which separates Baku from the Caspian these days. It is only when you look back along the concave curve of the promenade that you catch a glimpse of the rust and crumbling concrete that still lies below.

Around here these days, it seems to me, bright and shiny is good. The drab Soviet monstrosities of two hotels, the Azerbaijan and the Absheron, where I spent many a happy if slightly bizarre visit, and which watched like two godless angels over the austere grandeur of the German POW-built

Dom Soviet from either side, have been ceremonially flattened. In their place are new monstrosities, oceans of glass and curved balconies gleaming in the sun, each taunting the other across the massive *meydan*, or Public Square. I'm bigger than you! Yes but I'm *brighter* than you! Maybe, but I'm *richer* than you! Ah yes, but I'm *tackier* than you! There's no answer to that.

As you stand on this one spot, and cast your eye around, there must be a dozen new buildings of similar or even more bizarre dimensions and designs, each seeking to shout louder than the last. The straight lines of Soyuz conformity have vanished. In modern architecture, curves and shiny glass are the order of the day. Forget Dubai, Astana, New York and London's Square Mile. Here you have the Sail, the Slug, the Shard *and* the Gherkin, like a surreal nautical cabbage patch of the world's most flamboyant designs.

Only one hundred years ago the whole Bulvar had been reclaimed from the sea, using soil, trees and water that had to be transported from hundreds of kilometres away. (Oil tanker ships returning to Baku were taxed if they failed to bring soil back with them.) So it is hardly surprising that nothing is what it seems, and nothing quite seems to belong. It's as if the words genuine, natural, integral and indigenous have been suddenly and utterly banned from the city planners' dictionary. These are the words of an outdated concept, a discarded value, a rejected culture, and one which is no longer permitted to tabernacle in the New World of Baku. Now we must bow to the God of New Wealth; worship at the Temple of Façade. In repentance we must turn unreservedly from our previous sins of concrete and stone, dull and square, and must abandon ourselves instead to the glory of glass, shiny and curved. Now we must dance and sing a new song - the frenzied dervish and discordant scream of a new form of tacky materialism and keep-up-man-ship. Outside the Kremlin, over one thousand kilometres to the north, Lenin (had he been subject to a little less embalming, and not continuously displayed on a plinth for the world to gaze at and ponder at his fallen world of pseudo-equality), would have turned in his grave. The Zoroastrians would have combusted.

Gone are the comforting delights of the *tut* (mulberry), the apricot, the vine, the fig and the olive, which used to haphazardly line the tight bustling streets of old Baku, and from which the residents (including my mother-in-law) would contentedly sample the fruits. The gardens of the new promenade are now planted with giant Japanese bonsai, enormous Central American cacti, and two chunky rows of blackened palms, leading up to Debenhams (yes, Debenhams). According to the accompanying brass plate that gleams in the spring sun, the palms are Australian Xanthorrhoea, "Homeland: Australia; Age: 160-180 years old; Lifetime: 600 years; Planting date in the National Park: 23.12.2010." Japan, Australia, Mexico. Anywhere, everywhere, nowhere.

Disorientated, I sat on the (curved) park bench and looked over the Caspian. Diagonally across the bay, my eyes locked onto the largest of the many Azerbaijani flags that boldly announce to me which nation I am actually in. It hangs from what, at the time of writing, was the world's tallest flagpole; 156 metres. The wind tugs in strong gusts (some things never change). The flags wave nonchalantly, proudly, almost threateningly. Onto our promenade we will import the orient, the desert, the jungle, but never be in any doubt. We are Azerbaijan. The old babushka used to balance daily on her rickety balcony and shake the dust out of her Azerbaijani carpet. Today a new Azerbaijan stands on the shore of the Caspian, and appears to shake out the dust of anything classic, anything natural from her magnificent blue, red and green national flag.

I looked over my shoulder, inland, away from the Caspian, oblivious to the fact that within a few years this very street would become the start and finish line of a prestigious, annual Formula One race. Today this was merely the young Bakuvian man's race track they call Prospect Neftchilyar. Three huge white limousines screeched to a halt. Decked with pink, red and green plastic flowers, and metres and metres of frilly white lace, they looked as though they'd been driven at high speed through the aisles of a particularly flamboyant haberdashery superstore, and just emerged out the other side. Proud drivers stepped out of their status symbols, shoulders back, glowing with pride, brushing an invisible minuteness of fluff off their black trousers, their white shirts. Their sole purpose is to ensure that she whose big day it is should remain at all times the undisputed centre of attention. As for the bride, she knows she must remain secondary, a mere appendix to the one who is to be adored. It's the Chrysler, the X5 or the Audi. It is she that we dress up for, she that we obsessively protect from any speck of dust that might dare to alight upon her frame; it is she who radiantly transfigures before us in glorious white. It is she who steals the show. It's *her* day. Ask any man.

Once when self-consciously walking through the streets of Baku, I enquired of my Azerbaijani wife, "Why does everyone know I'm a foreigner?" She smiled and said nothing. "Yes, I know, but what if I wore the same black clothes, walked the same way, grew the same moustache, and dyed my hair black?" "No," she replied, calmly, knowingly, amused. "They'd still know." "But *why* would they know?" "It's the question marks in your eyes."

Thus I viewed the confusing world of a new Baku, through lenses of Eastern dust and Western question marks. And with that, I rose from my park bench (curved, chrome) and returned home to my mother-in-law's apartment (straight, stoical, sturdy, Stalinist), just four blocks back from the shore. And just one block in, I was back in real Baku. To the concrete, the *Khrushchyovka* (five-storey apartments built during the early 1960s) the dust, the garbage, the weeds, the flying plastic bags. To the gnarled and idle taxi drivers slumped half asleep in their rusting yellow *ghiguli* (Ladas); to the crumbling balconies, the shadowy alleys, the harsh graffiti. And to the honest corruption of hostile-looking men drinking *chai*, arguing and spitting on street corners. Many say that nostalgia is not what it used to be, but I think there's a great future in it. Whatever, I feel so much more at home here, one block in.

But some things will never change

We went to see the lawyer this morning. We needed to know the process for privatising Bela's former apartment from its Soviet collective history.

Walking through an old metal-framed glass doorway, we entered the world of the Baku *advokat*. Introducing ourselves to one of the lawyers, I avoided the temptation of grabbing his attention with my inside knowledge of his trade. "My grandfather used to work for Gotelee and Goldsmith, was the Ipswich Town FC solicitor from their amateur days right through to winning the First Division Championship in 1961-62 and beating AC Milan in Europe, was rumoured to have chosen their blue and white colours, and occasionally used to take me to watch a match in the director's box, including the famous match in 1964 when Sheffield Wednesday players famously fixed the game in what became known as the 'British betting scandal'. Actually." Although I've dined out on such prestigious history for years, somehow this morning, in this dingy office in Prospect Azadliq, Baku, I didn't think our man would be too impressed.

So instead I left Bela (and her sister Gula, who had come with us) to do the talking, while I sat silently with them and looked around. Behind six elderly wooden desks sat six elderly wooden solicitors - two women and four men. Each of the men wore dark suits and black shirts. Their desks were almost bare; no computer, no typewriter and no phone; just a single neat pile of documents and a tea cup. An ancient, wall-mounted angle-poise lamp hung above each desk. Clearly the desks had not moved in years. Nor had the lawyers. They just sat there, waiting. Waiting for punters, waiting for tea, waiting for their newspaper, waiting to go home, waiting to retire. Just waiting. Four of the lawyers would occasionally read their newspaper, then wearily put it down and spend the next five minutes staring straight ahead (one put her head in her folded arms and fell asleep). Then they would read a bit more.

Then suddenly, bizarrely, one of the men rose from his chair and ran rapidly across the room, disturbing an atmosphere that up till that moment had been on the lethargic side of rigor mortis. It was a shock to see such action – there was obviously a legal emergency that needed immediate and urgent attention. As my startled eyes followed this frenzied activity across the room, I realised the emergency was not so much legal as electric. One of the lawyers had forgotten to switch off his *kipyetelnic* (the electrical element for heating tea water in an individual cup), and the boiling water in his tea cup was spilling with bubbling ferment all over his ancient desk. After some fervent mopping up with some tissues, order was restored and the room returned to its slumber. And then a lady came in selling the latest copy of *Kriminal.*

While the idle lawyer at the next desk craned his ear to hear our story, we did our business in whispers with what transpired to be a kind and pleasant man in his 60s who, after wrongly guessing which of the women either side of me had accepted my hand in marriage, shook Bela's hand in congratulations. In response to the story of Bela's apartment, sometimes he was enraged, sometimes he was charming, always he was attentive. At the end of the session he withdrew from his pocket a pile of tiny cut slips of blank paper held together with a paper clip. Carefully withdrawing one piece of paper, he wrote the phone number of his office on it. This was his business card. He looked up and spoke with a twinkle in his eye. "I threw my mobile phone out 10 years ago." We paid him 10 Manat (about £7.72 at today's rates) for his 30-minute consultation.

As we left, he gave us one final word of advice. "You never make any progress, or really enjoy anything, unless you first have problems." With such advice, solicitors all over the world have made their fortunes.

CHAPTER THIRTEEN
KYRGYZSTAN

n 2010 I was invited to change my role within Samaritan's Purse once more. Over several years we had refined and defined our regional focus geographically, and I was asked to become the first overseas regional appointment of the UK office. I was now to earn my salary under the title of Regional Manager, Eastern Europe and Central Asia. My responsibility was to oversee the programmes to which Samaritan's Purse was committed in these two regions of the world, primarily in the wonderful countries of Azerbaijan, Belarus, Kyrgyzstan and Ukraine.

Since my first visit in 2001 (with Habitat for Humanity), I have returned to Kyrgyzstan over thirty times - more often than to any other country. Sharing borders with China, Kazakhstan, Tajikistan and Uzbekistan, Kyrgyzstan (or formally, The Kyrgyz Republic) is a spectacularly beautiful and mountainous country in Central Asia whose boundaries were forcibly created under Stalin's regime in the 1920s.

It is approximately the same size as Great Britain although, totally unlike the British Isles, 90% of the land area is at least 1,500m above sea level. Although two-thirds of the population is ethnically Kyrgyz, numerous other people groups inhabit the country, including Dungan, Russian, Tajik, Tatar, Uyghur and Uzbek.

With Gross Domestic Product (GDP) being estimated at $2,200 per capita, Kyrgyzstan jostled with its neighbour to the south-west, Tajikistan, for the dubious reputation of being the poorest country in Central Asia, and in the former Soviet Union. To put this figure in context, approximately twenty African countries have a higher GDP than The Kyrgyz Republic. The country is dangerously dependent on the remittances from overseas guest workers (e.g. those who go to work in Moscow cleaning streets and who send their earnings home). Unemployment and alcoholism are rife. The country rates very poorly on Transparency International's Corruption Perceptions Index, and with two revolutions in its short post-*perestroika* history, the nation remains politically and economically unstable.

Islam is the dominant religion, with regular examples of radical fundamentalist activity being exhibited in the south, and increasingly in the north, where the capital Bishkek is situated. Whilst many small church groups merely meet in homes, the very strict religious laws insist that churches wishing to formally register their existence should give the authorities full details of at least 200 members as part of the condition of registration. For the few churches that do gain registration, there are still tight restrictions relating to the activities they are allowed to pursue. A number of violent attacks have been made on church buildings and staff members in recent times, and some believers have been alienated from their communities by, for example, being forbidden from grazing their sheep, making purchases from the local shop, or even burying their dead in their own villages.

With significant and often poorly directed financial support from Westerners who were motivated by the collapse of the Soviet Union, the church in Kyrgyzstan had begun to see rapid growth in the decade following independence. Ministries were established and marketed, church buildings erected, and some pastors' salaries lavishly paid for. But the membership - and particularly the leadership - of the 1990s church in Kyrgyzstan primarily comprised Russian ethnic believers, and as the Kyrgyz authorities increasingly established their independence politically and culturally, large numbers of ethnic Russians felt frustrated by the glass ceilings, and left for Moscow or the West.

Because of local tensions, and the struggles that all young churches seem to encounter, the distractions and weariness of materialism and in-fighting set in, and missionaries (and NGOs) gradually pulled out. Many who wanted to stay were not permitted to (by immigration restraints), and the numbers of people coming to Christ reached a plateau. Due to the 2008 global economic downturn, more international Mission agencies struggled to maintain their previous financial support and pulled out of the region. At this time post-*perestroika* ethnic Kyrgyz believers were beginning to come of age, and had a growing realisation that they needed to find truly indigenous models of church in order to identify with the rapidly changing world around them.

Samaritan's Purse UK had worked in Kyrgyzstan since 2004, and this remains the only country where we invested significant time and resources into each of the three main building blocks of our work, namely children's ministry, emergency relief, and community development.

Having visited and loved this nation before I had even heard of Samaritan's Purse, I persuaded my colleagues to send Operation Christmas Child gift-boxes to Kyrgyzstan in the first year I joined the organisation. An average of over 70,000 gift boxes have been sent there in each of the subsequent years.

One day, whilst travelling through the country monitoring the gift-box programme, I was introduced to a couple who over the next decade would become extremely close friends and work colleagues. Pastor Dima and Irina Trofimov had been church-planting since they were 20 years old, and had developed an NGO that very successfully worked with homeless and vulnerable children. This eventually led the couple to becoming government advisors on the development of a national foster care policy. Dima and Irina invited us to bring a Discovery Team to Kyrgyzstan to renovate a building and run a summer camp in their home town.

Just at that time my colleagues and I were seeking to develop a programme to envision and equip local churches to reach out holistically to the most vulnerable families in their neighbourhood. And just at that time, Dima and Irina were frustrated that many good Christian initiatives in their society were happening *outside* of the structure of the church, for example through NGOs. Consequently only a few Christian activists ever became involved with social action in their communities, with the remainder of the church falsely comforting themselves that someone else was doing this. The couple longed to envision and equip churches in Kyrgyzstan to develop a more integral approach to mission. We therefore agreed to work together on a programme that would later become known as 'Raising Families'. Within a very short time this would become by far the most important, effective and fulfilling work I have ever done; one which reflects my most fundamental values and which defines all the years I spent with Samaritan's Purse.

We began in 2009 by visiting and mapping 170 churches right across the country. Each visit enabled us to get to know the state of the nation, the state of the church and each community a little bit better.

We met independent evangelical Pastor Zhengiz. A broad and jovial man, he arrived an hour late for our meeting, full of lavish apologies. "My brother was married this afternoon and I couldn't get away." After showing us around his church building just north of Bishkek, he took us on to another part of his parish – the Bishkek rubbish dump.

We were told that the city authorities had recently claimed this vast expanse of land as theirs due to its potential for raising taxes from the growing number of inhabitants who have made it their home.

On one side of the road is an informal new town, proudly named Tundik (the roof of a yurt) in honour of the now unaffordable traditional Kyrgyz home and, on the other side of the road, just short of the Kazakh border, is its twin informal settlement that had, as it turned out, a slightly more modest name.

"What is your town called?" I asked one resident. "Eighty-Four," was the reply. Assuming he thought I'd asked the age of his mother, I asked again. "Eighty-Four". The town is called Eighty-Four. *Vosem Desyat Chetiri* (Russian), or *Seksentor* (Kyrgyz).

Is it a town, or is it a rubbish dump? Well, it's both. The town of Eighty-Four has sprung up rapidly as more and more Kyrgyz people have become desperate for some income. They have come from all over the country in the hope of making a living selling scrap. Scrap plastic, scrap copper, scrap steel. But in the last year, the previously rising value of scrap had once more plummeted. We heard random, diverse quotes of scrap value. In truth, you get whatever you can get for the stuff today.

"How many people live in Eighty-Four?" I asked, bracing myself for the inevitable answer. "Five hundred," was the less obvious reply.

As the sun set on a barren wilderness of snow and waste, our car slipped and squirmed down the thick, muddy tracks that marked out semi-formal rows of mud-brick housing. I guess one in ten was occupied. The remainder appeared to be derelict or, maybe more promisingly, they functioned as boundary markers - a few courses of mud block awaiting completion when one day their owner would prosper. We were asked not to take photographs, at least not of the people.

Dumps have the same smell the world over. I've encountered them from the steaming heat of the Nicaraguan tropics to the wild and bitterly cold Roma communities of the Balkans and Eastern Europe. But here live the Kyrgyz, traditionally nomads who were more at home with livestock and mountains but, by landing abruptly at the tail end of globalisation, were currently forced to be recyclers - scavengers by another name. Admittedly, at one point we did have to wait while a herdsman steered his handful of sheep through the mud. And one could still just make out the dark mountains behind him, silhouetted beyond the rising mist. But here in Eighty-Four, on the whole, the livestock are rats and the mountains are rubbish.

Sliding crablike down to the bottom of a steep hill, and with a quick glance at the corresponding climb before us, our aging VW Passat decided enough was enough. It wasn't going back and it wasn't going on. In protest of the conditions, it kicked layers of mud and waste from under its wheel and, lurching sideways one more time, came to an undignified halt. We were stuck in a rut. Our driver, Artem, didn't seem too worried, and Zhengiz found it hilarious.

"No worries," he exclaimed, jumping gleefully out of the car, the shoes he had just worn to his brother's wedding instantly caked with mud. "There are five families of believers who live in Eighty-Four, and we've come to a halt just across the road from where one of the families lives. We'll visit them, and after the sun has set the mud will quickly freeze, and we'll be able to drive out again. No problem."

So that's what we did. We visited the little mud-walled home of Idbek and Sapargul, and their young daughter Nazira, who said nothing but snuggled affectionately between her Mama and the pastor, and stroked both their hands. There was no electricity, and the water standpipe was three very muddy kilometres away. Artem had pointed it out to us on the way into Eighty-Four. A few children from Eighty-Four even made it to school, we were told, albeit ten kilometres away. Idbek and Sapargul had been married for two years, Kyrgyz style (i.e. informally). They had both been married previously. They hoped to have one more child.

In appearance and stature she looked to be about eleven, but Nazira turned out to be 24. The family were delighted to invite their pastor and his foreign friends into their little home. But we ate and drank nothing. There wasn't anything *to* eat and drink. This family would not be eating tonight.

We asked them about where they had moved from, how business was these days, and what their dreams were. I'd learned over my 60-plus visits to former Soviet and Eastern bloc countries over the previous five years that this was always a good question to ask. However poor they were today, people still had dreams. But Idbek and Sapargul really didn't seem to understand the question at all. Artem and Zhengiz had to explain to them what we meant by dreams in at least four or five different ways, until it became quite embarrassing. It really did feel as though this was a family so poor that even hope was hopeless. Eighty-Four had seemingly rubbished whatever aspirations had once been nestling in their hearts.

Eventually Idbek began talking about transport. "I guess if I had a motorbike I would fetch water for my neighbours, take children to school, and run it as a taxi."

Waving goodbye, and thanking them for their hospitality, we walked across more mud, waste and snow towards a bonfire on the crest of the hill. Here we came across a small gaggle of boys and girls of about 18 to 20 years old, who were burning plastic and rubber casings off wire cable in order to extract the copper inside. Thick black smoke rose into the rapidly-darkening remains of the evening light. We warmed ourselves by the fire, trying to block out the dreadful stench of the burning materials, and chatted with these courteous young people for a few minutes about life in Eighty-Four.

As we left they apologised to Pastor Zhengiz. "We are sorry," they said. "We have sinned. Your visit has left us with a heavy conscience. We feel such shame living here and doing this job for a living. We're sorry."

Zhengiz was right. Less than 30 minutes after sunset the mud had frozen and, without a murmur, the old car obediently drove us off over the now solid waste and back into Bishkek, leaving the residents of Eighty-Four to another night of bitterly cold, powerless, waterless, dreamless regret.

How this Raising Families programme grew in the coming years will be the subject of the following chapter.

Samaritan's Purse remained ready to respond to natural and/or man-made disasters anywhere in the world, if ever and whenever such support is required. One such disaster, sadly caused by mankind, happened in Southern Kyrgyzstan in June 2010.

Following an uprising (the second in five years), the then President of Kyrgyzstan fled to the southern capital city of Osh. Here, on 10 June 2010, riots erupted between different ethnic groups, which resulted in the deaths of at least 400 people, and injuries to countless others. Up to 100,000 Uzbeks temporarily fled the city to escape the violence, and Samaritan's Purse responded to the crisis by sending food, medicines and toiletries. The response was mainly coordinated by Irina, and the goods were distributed by networks of local Christian believers across all the ethnic groups.

When I visited the city five weeks later, well after the international media had moved on, Osh was still in a terrible mess, with houses burned to the ground and thousands of people living homeless on the streets, terrified by the nightly, random atrocities and unspeakably violent attacks that were still being made on them. To one degree or another, there was evidence of violence perpetrated by all the main people groups, and Samaritan's Purse worked alongside all ethnicities, but the story that follows just happens to be from visits I made to Uzbek *Mahalla* (neighbourhoods) of Chereomushki.

> We drove with Pastor Ruslan through Chereomushki district, which was originally a Russian military area. This was one of the regions where the ethnic violence that ripped through Osh had the greatest impact. Whichever way we turned, home after home was burned out, and clusters of women crouched together by the roadside, staring at nothing and talking to one another in anxious tones. White and blue 18-square-metre UNHCR tents had arrived just that week; they were squeezed into the gardens and onto the courtyards of burned-out homes. One middle-aged man crouched by the road side rocking; with cigarette in hand he twitched violently and constantly.

131

We stopped and spoke with some of the women. "We were given food aid for a few days, but in the last few weeks we've been forgotten again," they said. "Can you give us some people to help us clean up? We don't believe anyone wants to help us anymore. All our documents have been burned. We went to the government office to seek help, but we were badly beaten up and we had to run for our lives for fear of being killed. We were given one mattress, one tent and five blankets, for six people."

Another woman told us that between them they'd created a makeshift district government to protect their rights and try to secure passports. "But the city government don't want to help us." The women were very respectful and pleasant to us. They just wanted us to stop and *listen*. Listen to their story. They didn't appear to be angry; just sad, deeply sad, broken, defeated; and still afraid.

As we drove on round the corner Ruslan suddenly stopped the car, jumping out to give a man in his early 40s a big hug in the street. "This is Botir! He's my car mechanic – the best one in town," he told us. A small crowd gathered, and Ruslan took some Pampers from the boot of his car and gave them to some of the young mums. They were extremely grateful and appreciative.

Botir invited us to climb through the charred gates of his burned-out home, waving his hand around the courtyard's thirteen rooms. "There were 15 of us living here." Apart from a UNICEF tent, only rubble and twisted metal remained. Steps led down to what was left of a burned-out basement. He showed us a blackened saucepan, over which was a lid. With a subtle mixture of anger, respect and functional pragmatism, he removed the lid. "These are the bones of my mother and my sister. We're still finding them in the rubble. In this basement I hid ten of my family. Seven of us survived. My brother draped himself over my mother and sister to shelter them, and he had burns all over his body. So he rushed across the road and jumped into the stream, then was taken to hospital. He definitely should have lived, but we were told he died overnight. We don't know who took his life."

He stopped for a moment to pour out some bottled water for us: three complete strangers from another culture. We each drank in turn from the one remaining cup. "My father built this house in 1960. My mother was an invalid – this was her chair." He gesticulated towards some twisted metal remains that were still identifiable as a wheelchair. "The house took three days to burn. In this district, 286 homes were burned and at least 1,000 died." His body language was unsettled, agitated, fitful. A woman had followed us in from the street. "This is my wife Guzal. Look at where she was beaten around the head. They poured petrol over her head but I dragged her into the house and hid her in the basement. That wound is 40 days old. She is a doctor but, because we were attending to my brother, she didn't even get to go to hospital." Irina held onto Guzal as she sobbed deeply. "We're still so afraid," said her husband. "We need the Russian army to come, like they did in 1990. We need them again now."

As we left Botir and the remains of his family, an old woman came hobbling up to greet us. "I hear you have some Pampers. May I have some? They killed my daughter-in-law, and the baby is now ten weeks old." We gave her some Pampers; she thanked us, and bustled off down the road again, through some rubble, and disappeared behind another burned-out gate.

A few days later we returned to the Chereomushki Mahalla to do a small non-food distribution with the final few thousand Som from the Samaritan's Purse donation, and met up with Botir again. He was our link man and Guzal was with him. She held onto Irina as a long-lost close friend, and wept some more fear out all over her.

Ruslan took some supplies to another quarter of the Mahalla, while Irina and I stayed and talked with a crowd of a dozen or so women. We gave them a choice. "Do you trust Botir, or do you want us to personally distribute to each family?" "Oh no, we trust our men completely to do the distribution fairly," they replied.

They then updated us on the troubles in Chereomushki. "Last night at about 5pm the military came again with guns," we were told by several of the women. Four out of a group of 10 women told us every detail. As they did so, fear, panic and strain seized their faces and their hands. They took intermittent breaks in their stories as they broke down into tears. As one old woman sat and shouted out her frustration onto whoever was listening, the others stood silently, listening and staring. "The military beat up some women, and took away three boys; one 19, another 15 and another 14. They forced off their finger nails, and demanded money for the boys' return. During the war they demanded $5,000 per boy, but this has now risen to $10,000. The family of the 19-year-old must have paid the money, because he was returned, but the other two have gone. When boys were taken previously, even if they were returned, they died soon afterwards because of the beatings and the shock. Those three days when they torched our houses were terrible, but these days it's even worse. They take one or two people away every time they visit, and this drip, drip, effect is killing us with fear."

"What have you eaten in the last 24 hours?" I asked. "Oh we're fine for food at the moment. We have noodles and flour. But winter's coming, and we're in tents, and our children have no roof over their heads. 50 of us women went down and protested at the government office yesterday, but they just sent us away."

After more hugs, we left to the sound of a sincere, impassioned and chilling final word from one of the women. "Tell them to come and kill us all in one go, not little by little like this."

We drove down Navayi Street to another district. Every home was burned out, as well as the small shops and bazaars, only some of which were still recognisable. One or two of these hard-working people had defied the odds and set up stalls on top of the rubble. I saw a butcher, a vegetable seller, and three men making a stove for baking and selling bread.

We drove through town, past the mysteriously-untouched Uzbek theatre, the burned-out Uzbek TV station, and onto Furkat district, huddled broken and distressed on either side of the main road to Jalalabad and Bishkek. Turning right into one section of the community, we drove a little way up the hill and round a bend in the dirt road.

Another gaggle of women gathered round the car, and invited us to visit their homes. We climbed through a window ("I'm sorry, but this the only way in now") into another spacious courtyard settlement, and chatted to four or five of the women who joined us. "This is Vasiba. Her husband was killed by a sniper." In better times Vasiba would have been tall, elegant. Today she just looked crushed, thin, limp, with eyes staring out into nowhere. "We were told to paint SOS on our houses for help," said one woman, "but all this did was to identify us as Uzbeks and we were attacked. If we go into town we are beaten, and everything is stolen from us."

It was then that we heard urgent shouting from down the road. Instantly the women were distracted from our conversation. Involuntarily they wrapped their clothes around them tightly, and wrung their hands together. The electric atmosphere reminded me of when there was the genuine threat of another Tsunami in Batticaloa, Sri Lanka, 30 days after the big one. An intense fear had gripped the women and they nervously opened a gate, just a little, onto the road. About 80 metres away, at the edge of the main road, a large crowd had gathered. One or two women went for a closer look, then returned and shouted in panic to Irina, "Hide your men! Hide your men! The police have taken some more of our men away. They put pins up their finger nails and demanded money." I was the only man in sight, Ruslan having gone further up the road to talk with another group; so they hid me behind a brick wall. Before long we carefully made our way back to Ruslan and to the car, the walled curve in the road shielding me from the police. Leaving these terrified women, we drove back to the main road. By the time we arrived there the police had left. A group of agitated but helpless-looking men stood where the action had been, shaking their heads and clenching their fists.

I asked Ruslan what he felt about living here these days with his family. (Ruslan is ethnically Russian but his wife is half Uzbek.) "We're going to stay," he said. "This is my nation. These are my people. Yes they hate. Yes, they are killers. But they're mine. I'm not going anywhere." And with that we crossed town again, to visit his church rehab centre situated in a village just south of Osh.

On our way we were stopped at a checkpoint. The Kyrgyz police asked a lot of questions and studied our passports, then let us go. The rehab centre housed Kyrgyz and Uzbek students until the war started, when almost all the Uzbeks decided that for security reasons they had to leave; 10 Kyrgyz students remained.

The staff member on duty this afternoon was Artiom, who is himself half Russian and half Uzbek. He had helped with the distribution of food, along with most of the students. On his way home one evening he had been stopped at the same road block we had just encountered; only he was beaten up and locked in a container. "You will wait here till 10.00pm," they told him, "and then we'll kill you, for breaking the curfew." He was saved when a military leader, who used to be his neighbour, recognised him and let him go.

Another team leader, Ulmaz, was on duty the night the war started ('war' is the expression that Ruslan uses). That night his wife, daughter and son disappeared. The son's body was found 10 days later, after Ulmaz had gone to the neighbours who had killed him and begged them to tell him where they had dumped him. His wife was finally identified by her wedding ring; his 14-year-old daughter by her earring. He has a three-year-old daughter who now clings to him constantly. And he's started drinking again.

Ruslan had had enough for one day. He was distant, distracted and restless as we slowly drove home. I asked him if the rehab centre received any help from overseas. "Huh!" he exclaimed. "No. We put together a proposal with USAID, and they did give us minimal support. But they were so anti-Christian." Then, without warning, he stopped the car in its tracks, and looked intensely, straight into my eyes. "You know, we *could* work with the UN but, Alan, this is my first experience of war, and I'm still under depression. We used to feed the homeless, twenty of them each Sunday, but we just haven't managed to start doing this again. We can't preach the gospel if we do stuff with the UN. You've got to understand, Alan. I've never felt such *awful*, terrible fear before – *horror*! You just can't do anything." He then started the engine, and we drove off home, quietly. Even I had no more questions.

CHAPTER FOURTEEN

RAISING FAMILIES

My disaster response experiences were not limited to Sri Lanka and Kyrgyzstan. For a couple of years I managed Samaritan's Purse UK International Disaster Response programme. Usually this involved recruiting and sending experts (in sectors such as health, security, and water and sanitation) on short-term assignments into disaster zones. It was at the time of the Ebola crisis in West Africa, which necessitated me having some very close liaison, and the developing of returnee protocols with, Public Health England and Public Health Wales, as those who I had sent were working directly alongside our two American colleagues, Dr Kent Brantly and Nancy Writebol, who became global news after contracting Ebola in Liberia in 2014. Also in 2014 I spent time with our flood response teams in Serbia and Bosnia, and in 2015 I was in Nepal (after the earthquakes), in Northern Iraq (with the Yazidi refugees following the ISIS uprising), and I also walked with the Syrian refugees through Southern Europe.

Be it about being flown over the magnificent Himalayas at the crack of dawn by a 21-year-old helicopter pilot in Nepal, or of seeking UN permission to land a Samaritan's Purse plane on a mined beach, or of the extraordinarily bizarre meeting I had with the global head of the Yazidi people, many more stories could be told from these visits. But however urgent the need, and however practical and logistical the task, the roles that I always seemed to thrive on were more pastoral and relational in nature. Whilst my colleagues had the adrenaline rush of installing massive water filtration units in jungles, triaging and operating on injured victims of war in temporary field hospitals, or arranging for plane-loads of supplies to land in the dead of night on obscure landing strips controlled by rebel armies, the most productive times I personally had in terms of disaster response was when I could mobilise and work through networks of local churches. Some church groups were too fragmented, or not well enough connected with their communities, or in other ways ill-equipped to respond to emergencies. However, I found that with a little patience, some hastily delivered training, and through me introducing them and commending them to the UN cluster teams, these 'here today, *here* tomorrow' teams of local Christ-followers had a great, holistic and long-term role to play, long after the emergency teams had left. I concluded that I do important better than I do urgent. I probably do steady state better than I do emergency; development better than I do relief.

I love to work alongside those local churches around the world that want to engage meaningfully with their society, unite across confessions, lead many people to Christ, and see holistic transformation in the lives of the poorest and most marginalised families in their communities. Raising Families, which is often quite accurately described as a Church and Community Mobilisation (CCM) programme, does exactly that, and is a great example of a church-based programme that is committed both to social action *and* to seeing dozens of people coming to Christ every week. To manage the Raising Families programme consumed my final years with Samaritan's Purse, and without a doubt this was the most fulfilling and effective role of my employment with them.

I believe that as the main agent of the Kingdom of God on earth, the local church has been equipped by God to fulfil a compassionate, Christ-centred mission to its community and neighbourhood. Through a practical commitment to envisioning, encouragement, training, mentoring and support, the church can fulfil The Great Commission (Matthew 28:19-20) to make disciples, and to demonstrate the holistic gospel that Jesus proclaimed in the synagogue in Nazareth (Luke 4:18-19), i.e. the lifting of people from poverty, be it spiritually, physically (in terms of health and wealth), emotionally, relationally and societally. This envisioning and mobilising of churches in their communities is precisely what Raising Families offered.

Whilst being developed as a global model, Raising Families was tailored to be appropriate to each culture and context, and their different social, economic and legal frameworks. Having functioned successfully through experienced partners in Central Asia and in Africa since 2006, a decade later we had refined the Raising

Families model, and the programme was serving 1,870 local churches from many denominations, strengthening those churches in the proclamation and demonstration of the gospel of Jesus Christ. Denominations and churches that used to compete with one another were now working together in harmony for the sake of the Kingdom of God.

So how did it work? Well, Raising Families national partners provided envisioning and training, after which responsive church members from each church formed a Church Action Group (CAG). These CAGs firstly assessed both the needs and the assets of their community, and then committed to working with a minimum of twenty of their most vulnerable neighbouring families, supporting their development in terms of health, education, livelihoods, shelter and protection. Consequently, those 1,870 churches enabled over 40,000 families to benefit from this programme. Sometimes broader, more general community activities and interventions such as environmental clean ups, providing access to markets, schools and health services, and improving water supplies became significant by-products of this process.

In one such community, the church developed a town-wide reputation for being an effective resource for the homeless poor (adults and children), and in another, a rehabilitation programme rescued and met the needs of those trapped in the despair of drug and alcohol misuse. Elsewhere, a *subodnik* (a Saturday morning programme to clean up the local park) - undertaken by eight churches uniting together - resulted in the city's environmental officer being so impressed that he asked ten of the poorest volunteers to report to him for employment on the following Monday morning.

To demonstrate its evangelistic impact in recent years, over three thousand people each year came to Christ as a direct result of the Raising Families programme. I would also regularly receive reports of CAGs naturally and effectively multiplying into neighbouring villages, and therefore rejoiced in the assumption that even more families encountered Christ through the impact of the programme. Not wanting that to remain an anecdotal assumption, we returned to survey churches that had completed the programme at least 18 months previously, and found that for every one hundred churches that had been envisioned through Raising Families, there were now 158 churches rolling out its training and practices.

The intelligent commitment of lead bishops and pastors within the participating denominations, and the provision of excellent facilitators proved to be key components for the success of the programme. Delivering excellent value for money, Raising Families worked so well because it was a prayer- and Bible-based programme, locally owned and implemented by the church and its neighbours, and relied not on external hand-outs, but on the resources that were already available in the community.

Nothing is built or established unless God gives it life, and to Him be all the glory. If God continues to bless this process as He has done so far, and on the basis of monitoring and evaluation already conducted on a large number of completed programmes, I can confidently anticipate that wherever this programme continues to exist, approximately twenty families per church will see significant, practical, quantifiable improvements to their lives: sickness averted, children in school, crops in the field and food on the table, and (on average) 60 people per week will continue to come through repentance and faith into a living relationship with God through Jesus Christ.

So having started with Samaritan's Purse on the management and distribution of children's gift boxes internationally, then developing a Short Term Mission Teams' programme, and then for a while having oversight of the International Disaster Relief programme, in my last few years I exclusively worked as Raising Families Programme Manager. In the early days we did some envisioning with churches in Azerbaijan, Belarus and Ukraine, but the programme really took off in Kyrgyzstan, Rwanda, Swaziland, Uganda and Zambia. It was mainly to these countries that my more recent and repeated visits took me, and where I witnessed so many people coming to Christ, and so much evidence of the Kingdom of God.

In 2017 Raising Families was chosen to be the Spring Harvest main stage Mission of Choice, which among other things involved us needing to select just one family from the 40,000 we worked with, who could feature with the Spring Harvest leaders in a promotional video. We worked for months to decide which nation, which region, which village, which church and then which family to select. There were literally thousands of families who could have told their stories to great effect. We finally selected wife and mother Emelienne, and she has become a bit of a star! Not only was her story filmed and broadcast to thousands of people at Spring Harvest, and on the internet, but I continue to hear stories from churches and families in several other countries about the impact her testimony has had on them.

Emelienne lives with her husband and six children in the village of Musenyi, in the very rural Anglican parish of Gahombo in Rwanda. The sun burned with intensity as she shared her transformative story outside her mud-brick house.

Before her church received envisioning and training through the Raising Families programme, their lives could only be described as hopeless. Finding food and school fees proved extremely difficult, and all the children had significant dietary problems. Having no funds to pay for health insurance, they were also excluded from access to even the most basic of health care. Rather than being an income generator, the fruit from the two lemon trees on the land around their little home was casually picked by random passers-by.

Then Emelienne was sent as the representative of her church to the Raising Families trainings. Envisioned and motivated, she returned to her village and helped form a Church Action Group (CAG) of seven members. Determined to see God's holistic transformation in their neighbourhood, the group first assessed their community's needs and their assets, and then selected and committed to 20 of the most vulnerable families in their village. Together they met every two weeks to pray, read the Bible, and save together; firstly 600 RWF and then 1,000 RWF (about 96p) per month. They took occasional jobs when they could, like gardening, cleaning, and selling other people's harvests, and invested those funds into the savings group as well.

"When we were trained in recognising and using our assets, I realised I could harvest the lemons from my two lemon trees. I netted 5,000 RWF from the first harvest, and I realised that if I could multiply the number of trees I had, then my income would grow accordingly. So I borrowed from the savings group and bought 22 more lemon trees. We are now on our third harvest from these 24 trees (two harvests per year), and each harvest brings in 50,000 RWF. I gave some lemon seedlings to my neighbours and trained them up. Now I buy their produce back and sell it at Kigali market, together with their banana, avocado and tree tomato harvests. God has blessed us simply and abundantly, and all from what we already had! Now I have started five other CAGs through other local churches of different denominations, and am also saving in one of these, as well as through another micro-finance arrangement."

"The training was more than eye-opening; it was revolutionary," declared Emelienne with modest confidence. "As a result of these initiatives my children go to school, their diet has improved, and we all have medical insurance."

After saving regularly for two years, the group agreed to invest into livestock for each family. Every family now has a goat. However, the group isn't there just to get rich, but the blessings they receive, they share with the village in Jesus' Name. So far they have built five houses for homeless families, and villagers are taking note and asking them where their motivation comes from.

"So far this year we have twelve new believers in our village, and ten others have returned to their faith. This alone is our encouragement to carry on working hard. But God also encouraged us from Revelation 2:9, when he said, "I know that you are poor, yet you are rich!" and 2 Corinthians 6:10, where we can say with Paul, "We are poor, yet making others rich.""

I have written elsewhere and at length about Raising Families, including a workbook called 'Raising Families: Core Values and Practices', which is a series of studies designed for the UK church to learn from these churches in Central Asia and Africa (see my website, cuttingacross.com, for more on this).

And we have much to learn from them. Not many churches in the UK have such a dynamic and strategic approach. Some British churches I have attended have quite obviously lost all understanding of why God has placed them as salt and light in their community. For them the church is the building (not, if pressed, in their formal theology, but definitely in the daily language they use, and therefore in reality). They have what I have referred to as a 'meetings and buildings' approach, by which I mean that virtually all their energies, resources, time and money is invested into events, meetings, gatherings and property. Their understanding (if it exists at all) is that the community needs to be attracted to come to *them*, to their meetings, to their buildings; not they to the community. Although Jesus urges us to sow ourselves into the ground and die (John 12:24), effectively giving up the power, through our attractional approach to our neighbours we continue to keep a tight and controlling hold of the reins. We have made a fundamental realignment of the Great Commandment, from 'Go' to 'Come', and we are mystified as to why the community finds it so hard to cross the threshold of our buildings, and to understand what it is we do within them.

The problem with this attractional approach really should be obvious. We ask people to remove themselves from the environment they know and from all their typical points of reference. We ask them to disconnect themselves from their post-modern world-view, and step into our mysterious world where we will inflict upon them our ancient (or modern) rituals, language and dress code, where they will be talked *at* (preached to) with little if any chance of debate or discussion, where they will be asked to sing songs (which outside of the football stadium, the music festival and the bath, they haven't done since school days), and where they will have to relate to people of different ages and cultures from themselves. And (if they arrive on a particular Sunday morning in the month) they could even be invited to participate (or asked *not* to participate, depending on our theology and practice) in the eating of flesh and the drinking of blood. No wonder most people would rather spend their Sunday morning walking in the park, shopping or cleaning their car!

Consequently, and despite the serious opposition and resistance they sometimes faced, many of the churches I worked with through Raising Families concluded that a church model consisting merely of meetings and buildings just didn't work. They could no longer just expect the community to come to them; they had to go to the community.

They also realised that the world would not be transformed by their preaching alone, and growing numbers of pastors and church leaders once more heard God's call to love their neighbours as themselves, and started investing into social action and mercy programmes. And as they began to do this, they came to another realisation - transformation would not happen through practical hand-outs alone. They began to see that, experienced as they were as *preachers* and deliverers of *mercy (aid)*, now they had to grow up in their understanding of both *discipleship* and of *development*, and of the strong link between the two. Thus the hand out became a hand up.

So Raising Families was an envisioning, training and support programme, led and managed by nationals in each country of operation, which supported church leaders and activists to learn a more integral approach to their mission; how to come alongside their neighbours in humility, to listen to them as well as to talk to them, to encourage them to be architects of their own futures, and to serve alongside them as agents of change.

My friends and colleagues in Central Asia and Africa went to churches of many denominations; churches that were hungry for change. Where invited, they led a programme of envisioning, firstly with the pastors, and then with church activists selected and approved by those pastors. Such activists (sometimes from different local churches) then formed themselves into Church Action Groups or clusters, and through listening to various people within their neighbourhoods got to know much deeper and better the heartbeat, hopes and fears, aspirations and frustrations, and the needs and assets of their local community.

Some of them then did a few seed projects (simple visual actions such as the street cleaning previously mentioned, or house repairs for the elderly) using their own resources, skills and capabilities, through which they gained confidence and exposure to the community. The lessons they learned through these simple initiatives were drawn out, honed and maximised through further training and support, and the Action Groups then grew in their capacity to be able to deliver more sustainable programmes of support and mentoring to the most vulnerable families in their village or neighbourhood.

Church Action Groups then learned how to work together with their local authorities, and how to put together project proposals and access external funding, thus developing small businesses for income generation, and drug and alcohol rehabilitation centres. In these ways the participating local churches became a driver of physical and spiritual transformation, bringing a holistic and tangible hope to people's lives and localities.

It was a great joy and privilege for me to spend my final five years with Samaritan's Purse serving these churches and communities, and many times I had to pinch myself to believe that such a normal person, without enormous confidence, education or charisma, but rescued by God, could be caught up to serve in such a dynamic expression of His Kingdom.

CHAPTER FIFTEEN

HOME

I t's an interesting stage of life, becoming a grandfather, being regarded as retired, and knowing that I have already lived longer than my father and, for that matter, the average age of my grandfather, great and great-great grandfather.

But, however many years I have left, I still have many dreams and ambitions. I love my family, I am part of a great church, I have enjoyed the best job in the world, and I love life. I don't understand eternity too well, even as I get older, but I know whom I have believed, and am utterly convinced that He is able to guard what I have entrusted to Him until that day when I see Him face to face. In the meantime, I want to keep living in God's fullness here on earth. I want to see every member of my family discover Christ and complete their lives under His Lordship, being at peace with God, ever growing in His love and grace, and living in harmony with one another. I want to be a culture-former, a teacher, an enabler, and to 'equip the saints for the work of ministry'. I want to visit more countries and write more books. I want to love my home, tend our garden, watch some football and walk along Felixstowe promenade with my wife. I want to live well, serve well and pray well. I want my life, my thinking, my relationships and my values to reflect the integral and abundant life that Jesus died to give us. Whatever our hand finds to do, let's do it with all our hearts. I want to end well.

I recall a woman once telling a famous preacher that she prayed for him daily, and particularly she prayed that before his life was through, all his dreams would be fulfilled. He was horrified. "Please don't pray that," he replied. "On the day I die, I still want to be dreaming dreams; to be having healthy ambitions. I want to die in faith." I feel the same, and am reminded of Hebrews 11, which records 'all these people were still living by faith when they died.'

People still ask me which my favourite country is. Others phrase it a little differently. "Where's your favourite destination?" There's only one answer to this, and that's 'Home'. For one who is such a traveller, I always love putting the key into the lock of my own front door. If travel were ever to become an escape from the reality of home, then something would be very wrong.

I love the same sort of household that Jesus loved – the one where Martha, Lazarus and Mary lived. We read about it in John chapter 12, when Jesus was invited to dinner in celebration of the fact that He'd just raised Lazarus from the dead.

It was actually a very attractive environment – really good friends celebrating an amazing event together. A bit like the parties that beautiful people apparently go to, and which much of the world jealously watches on music videos and Martini adverts. A place to which, we are told, we would all like to be invited, accepted, gathered up, included.

Imagine Martha. Sleeves rolled up, she's in the kitchen. OK, she can get a bit wound up at times, and she remembers with a coy smile the day that Jesus had a word with her about that. She'd listened well, and His word had been transforming. As a result, tonight she's in her element. She's been working away all day in order to prepare the very best food for the dinner party, and she's loved every minute of it. She would really like to be mingling with the guests too, but tonight Martha knows she has a job to do and, despite the sacrifice, and refusing to feel left out, she joyfully accepts the responsibility. She brings out another plate of food and places it near to Lazarus, who is reclining at table with Jesus.

Lazarus gets up, takes the plate, and begins meandering around the room, networking, relating; oozing with radiant joy out of his massive gratitude for the miracle of life. At the same time he listens attentively to his guests, expressing genuine interest in the comparatively mundane anecdotes of their week. "More orange squash, anyone? Quiche? Cheesy dips?" (Well, it is a *Christian* party remember).

Imagine a latecomer, tumbling in straight from work, hastily removing his coat, rushing into a deep conversation with someone he knows, and absent-mindedly grabbing a fistful of food from the passing tray. "Oh cheers mate." Then he looks up in mid-sentence, sees Lazarus and, utterly stunned, stops in his tracks. "Blimey, Lazarus, I thought you were dead." Recovering a little, he adds, "Hey mate, I'm sorry I didn't make the funeral. I was *so* busy. You know how it is. I'd just bought a field and had to go and view it. I'd just bought five yoke of oxen and had to take them for a test drive. Oh, and I'd just got married as well. Anyway, how did it go? Although I suppose you wouldn't really know, would you? Err, feeling any better now?"

Precisely at this moment an incident takes place that radically transforms the evening. Mary, spontaneously, shockingly prepared to break with the cultural norm for the greater good, takes half a litre of pure nard [*Himalayan plant: a perennial aromatic plant of the valerian family. Flowers: pinkish-purple. Native to: Himalayan range. Latin name Nardostachys jatamansi*], costing the equivalent of a year's wages, elegantly kneels down, and simply pours it over Jesus' feet. The buzz of conversation plummets like a stone and, in the deafening silence, the whole building instantly fills with the amazing fragrance of the perfume. You could cut the atmosphere with a knife.

Undeterred, unhurried, and with *such* grace, Mary then loosens her hair, stoops even further down, and wipes Jesus' feet - with her hair! Guests involuntarily place their hands over their mouths and faces, totally shocked and embarrassed. They exchange panicked glances at one another, wondering just what on earth has got into the normally sweet and modest Mary. These were the flagrant and suggestive actions of a prostitute, and yet she seemed totally oblivious of the fuss she was causing. There was nowhere for the guests to hide. This was just so wrong, so un-cool, such a cultural *faux pas. So* embarrassing.

It was Judas who broke the silence. He was *angry.* "*Why?* Why wasn't this perfume sold, and the money given to the poor?" And with deep frustrated rage, he clasped his hands together behind his neck and shouted into the sky, "It was worth *a year's wages!*"

He didn't say this because he cared about the poor, but because he was a thief. As keeper of the money bag, he used to help himself to what was put into it.

Every one of the disciples had had their suspicions about Judas, but at this moment of time that just didn't matter. They weren't thieves, but on this occasion they actually all completely *agreed* with Judas. There wasn't an Englishman among them, but even these flamboyant Middle Eastern guys were just too cultured, too conventional, too ordered, too functional even to *dream* of accepting that such a thing could be happening right before their eyes.

Because she was in the kitchen, Martha didn't actually witness the incident, but she clearly sensed the sudden change of atmosphere, and came through to see why the strong aroma. And Lazarus? Well, he was just happy to be alive. He thought his younger sister's gift was just brilliant. His head buzzed with praise, joy, laughter, awe. But of their guests, no one could even begin to cope with this ridiculous, overwhelmingly lavish act of celebratory worship that Mary had innocently poured out onto the Son of God.

No one, that is, except Jesus. There had been no hint of embarrassment from Him. In fact at that moment He decided that in the following days *He* would wash His *disciples'* feet, knowing full well that once more they would react all over the place. He could just imagine it. "You'll never wash *my* feet!" But here, tonight, at the dinner given in His honour, He comfortably received exactly this same treatment. It just didn't matter that this was usually an act of extreme sensuality, or that the guests, to a man, had just been blasted further outside their comfort zone than they'd ever been before. Jesus relaxed, Jesus received, Jesus accepted, Jesus enjoyed. And Jesus replied. "Leave her alone, Judas. It was intended that she should save this perfume for the day of my burial. You will always have the poor among you, but you will not always have me."

I love the way this family functioned so holistically together. In this story – in this family - we see task, team and individual. We see service, relationship and intimacy. Martha served, Lazarus related, Mary worshipped. Martha worked, Lazarus networked, Mary celebrated. Martha worked like she didn't need the money. Lazarus loved like he'd never been hurt. And Mary danced like no one was watching.

But that's my final point; people *were* watching. This family, this home church, this missional community wasn't a clique, a members-only club, a gated neighbourhood, a party purely for the beautiful people or the socially acceptable. This family was prepared to live in the spotlight, welcoming into their home not only Jesus and a few close friends to celebrate with them, but also cynics and thieves and critics and crowds, and even persecutors.

I'd like to have a holistic life like that. I'd like to be a part of an integrated family like that. I'd like to be a part of a local church like that. I'd like to be a part of a local community like that, and - this one takes a lot of faith – I'd like to be a part of a *nation* like that.

My wife Bela is a great *servant* and great *worshipper*, whereas I'm well into *service* and *relationship,* but I don't *celebrate* very well. As someone once sadly observed, "We are so often caught up in our activities that we tend to worship our work, work at our play, and play at our worship."

But here in Bethany we see a family getting the whole thing working together – serving, relating, worshipping - in comfortable, integral, natural, holistic interaction. They each accepted one another, and gladly supported and released one another to be what God had built them to be. They let the air of abundant life blow through them, they took risks, and they honoured Jesus as the centre of their universe.

Through pain and rebuke, Martha had learned a new way of serving. No longer was she into serving obsessively – tensing everyone else up by insisting on doing everything herself and not letting anyone else help her, but then whinging and becoming resentful when they didn't.

Jesus showed everyone during the following days what it takes to serve (John 13:1-17). You have to *settle* some things inside you, to *know* some things for certain. Jesus knew He had come from God. He knew He was going back to God. And He knew what the Father had placed in His hands. He knew His genesis. He knew His destiny. And He knew His assignment. Consequently He loved His disciples to the very end, by stripping Himself (v4), by serving them individually (v5-6), and by leaving them an example (v12-17).

And Lazarus wasn't into a selfish, egotistic model of networking for personal gain. He wasn't full of his own self-importance. He knew how to relate, to reach out, to befriend, to dialogue. Or maybe you think 'reclining at table' was a cosy little number for Lazarus. Typical bloke! Well, read verses 10-11 again. "Many came to see Lazarus..., so the chief priests made plans to kill (him) as well (as Jesus), for on account of (Lazarus) many were going over to Jesus and putting their faith in him." The way Lazarus *lived,* and the way Lazarus *spoke,* brought many to Jesus. We need men who have been raised up to new life and are grateful for it, who are comfortable with themselves and who they are, who don't lose themselves in practical service alone, but who know how to relate openly, confidently and humbly to others, to men *and* to women, and who know how to lead others to Christ.

As for Mary, well! This was far from mindless emotionalism and flamboyant exhibitionism. This was sheer worship, a celebration in spirit and in truth. Was she out of her mind? Well, yes actually. As Paul said to the Corinthian church, "If we are of sound mind, it's for you, but if we are beside ourselves, it's for God." There is a time for training and instructing people, but there's also a time for praising and worshiping God. But I think almost every one of us would have struggled with the extreme *extent* of Mary's generous worship, not because we're thieves, but because we are so *functional*. And we hide behind this functionality, justifying it with our muttered, principled conclusions that the poor could have benefitted more. But our principles can be so hypocritical, unless of course you *have* recently given a year's wages to the poor. So I think we'd better learn to cope with Mary's generosity, either now, or when we stand before His throne, where, according to what I read in the book of Revelation, worship is a *little* more than the singing of a few songs on a Sunday morning.

"Then I saw a Lamb, looking as if it had been slain, standing in the centre of the throne, encircled by the four living creatures and the elders. He had seven horns and seven eyes, which are the seven spirits of God sent out into all the earth. He came and took the scroll from the right hand of him who sat on the throne. And when he had taken it, the four living creatures and the twenty-four elders fell down before the Lamb. Each one had a harp and they were holding golden bowls full of incense, which are the prayers of the saints. And they sang a new song:

You are worthy to take the scroll and to open its seals, because you were slain, and with your blood you purchased men for God from every tribe and language and people and nation. You have made them to be a kingdom and priests to serve our God, and they will reign on the earth.

Then I looked and heard the voice of many angels, numbering thousands upon thousands, and ten thousand times ten thousand. They encircled the throne and the living creatures and the elders. In a loud voice they sang:

'Worthy is the Lamb, who was slain, to receive power and wealth and wisdom and strength and honour and glory and praise!'

Then I heard every creature in heaven and on earth and under the earth and on the sea, and all that is in them, singing:

'To him who sits on the throne and to the Lamb be praise and honour and glory and power, for ever and ever!' The four living creatures said,

'Amen,' and the elders fell down and worshiped." (Revelation 5:6-14 NIVUK)

This makes even a year's worth of perfume look a little dull, eh?

And so I say again; let's work like we don't need the money, love like we've never been hurt, and let's dance like no one's watching.

CuttingAcross.com is Alan Cutting's website.   On it you can find his other publications, blogs and videos, as well as photos he has taken around the world, and podcasts of talks he has given.   Alan is also a freelance consultant on church and community development programmes around the world.

30741129R00096

Printed in Poland
by Amazon Fulfillment
Poland Sp. z o.o., Wrocław